Tea & Scones

Tea & Scones

The Ultimate Collection *of* Recipes for Teatime

EXPANDED EDITION

hm | books

EDITOR *Lorna Reeves*

CREATIVE DIRECTOR/PHOTOGRAPHY *Mac Jamieson*

ART DIRECTOR *Cailyn Haynes*

ASSOCIATE EDITOR *Betty Terry*

COPY EDITOR *Nancy Ogburn*

EDITORIAL ASSISTANT *Janece Maze*

STYLIST *Lucy W. Herndon*

CONTRIBUTING STYLISTS *Lindsey Keith Kessler, Amy Burke Massey, Yukie McLean*

SENIOR PHOTOGRAPHERS *John O'Hagan, Marcy Black Simpson*

PHOTOGRAPHERS *Jim Bathie, William Dickey, Stephanie Welbourne*

CONTRIBUTING PHOTOGRAPHERS *Sarah Arrington, Kimberly Finkel Davis, Kamin H. Williams*

RECIPE DEVELOPER/FOOD STYLIST *Janet Lambert*

CONTRIBUTING RECIPE DEVELOPERS/FOOD STYLISTS *Aimee Bishop, Virginia Hornbuckle, Chantel Lambeth, Rebecca Treadwell Spradling, Loren Wood*

SENIOR DIGITAL IMAGING SPECIALIST *Delisa McDaniel*

DIGITAL IMAGING SPECIALIST *Clark Densmore*

hm
hoffmanmedia

CHAIRMAN OF THE BOARD/CEO *Phyllis Hoffman DePiano*

PRESIDENT/COO *Eric W. Hoffman*

PRESIDENT/CCO *Brian Hart Hoffman*

EVP/CFO *Mary P. Cummings*

EVP/OPERATIONS & MANUFACTURING *Greg Baugh*

VP/DIGITAL MEDIA *Jon Adamson*

VP/EDITORIAL *Cindy Smith Cooper*

VP/ADMINISTRATION *Lynn Lee Terry*

Hoffman Media, LLC
1900 International Park Drive
Suite 50
Birmingham, AL 35243
hoffmanmedia.com

ISBN 978-1-940772-26-4
Printed in China

ON THE COVER: Blueberry Tea Scones (page 21), Herbed Scones (page 85), and Hazelnut Scones (page 41)
Food styling by Janet Lambert
Photography by Kamin H. Williams | Styling by Lucy W. Herndon

VANILLA-PEAR SCONES
(recipe on page 103)

Contents

Introduction

SCONES. The mere mention of this baked good conjures up memories of times well spent enjoying afternoon tea. James Norwood Pratt in his eponymous *Tea Dictionary* contends that tearooms in the Western Hemisphere are judged by the quality of the scones they serve. In truth, a great scone can make almost any afternoon-tea menu enjoyable, whether elaborate and elegant or as simple as a cream tea.

One hundred and five recipes for a wonderful array of scones and spreads fill the 135 pages of this expanded and updated edition, originally published in 2011 under the title *Scones & Tea*. Plain scones, as well as sweet, savory, and gluten-free varieties, developed by our own talented food stylists and by select tearooms will all delight your taste buds. Some scones have accompanying spread recipes, while others are scrumptious with any one of the several butters, creams, curds, and other toppings presented in the last chapter.

For those who might consider scone-making an art to be mastered and are daunted by it, we have included a section of step-by-step photographs as a visual reference to demonstrate the necessary techniques for preparing the best scones possible. (Additional how-tos are available in video format at *teatimemagazine.com.*)

And since a delectable scone deserves an equally delicious tea to accompany it, we have provided two helpful guides—one for tea pairings and the other for steeping. We hope that as you sip our properly prepared recommendations, you'll discover a new favorite tea and that as you sample the many flavorful scone options herein, you'll uncover a treasure trove of delightful additions to your tea table.

CHERRY-ROSE SCONES
(recipe on page 41)

Tea-Steeping *Guide*

The quality of the tea served at a tea party is as important as the food and the décor. To be sure your infusion is successful every time, here are some basic guidelines to follow.

WATER

Always use the best water possible. If the water tastes good, so will your tea. Heat the water on the stove top or in an electric kettle to the desired temperature. A microwave oven is not recommended.

TEMPERATURE

Heating the water to the correct temperature is arguably one of the most important factors in making a great pot of tea. Pouring boiling water on green, white, or oolong tea leaves can result in a very unpleasant brew. Always refer to the tea purveyor's packaging for specific instructions, but in general, use 170° to 195° water for these delicate tea types. Reserve boiling (212°) water for black and puerh teas, as well as herbal and fruit tisanes.

TEAPOT

If the teapot you plan to use is delicate, warm it with hot tap water first to avert possible cracking. Discard this water before adding the tea leaves or tea bags.

TEA

Use the highest-quality tea you can afford, whether loose leaf or prepackaged in bags or sachets. Remember that these better teas can often be steeped more than once. When using loose-leaf tea, generally use 1 generous teaspoon of dry leaf per 8 ounces of water, and use an infuser basket. For a stronger infusion, add another teaspoonful or two of dry tea leaf.

TIME

As soon as the water reaches the correct temperature for the type of tea, pour it over the leaves or tea bag in the teapot, and cover the pot with a lid. Set a timer—usually 1 to 2 minutes for whites and oolongs; 2 to 3 minutes for greens; and 3 to 5 minutes for blacks, puerhs, and herbals. (Steeping tea longer than recommended can yield a bitter infusion.) When the timer goes off, remove the infuser basket or the tea bags from the teapot.

ENJOYMENT

For best flavor, serve the tea as soon as possible. Keep the beverage warm atop a lighted warmer or under your favorite tea cozy if necessary.

Tea-Pairing Guide

CHOOSING A TEA that perfectly complements the menu for afternoon tea is a critical part of hosting a successful event. When selecting infusions to accompany scones, keep in mind that the flavor of the tea should enhance—rather than compete with or overpower—the flavors and mouthfeel of these teatime treats, and vice versa. For that reason, we recommend reserving delicate teas, such as the whites, for drinking on their own. Greens, blacks, and many oolongs are excellent choices for serving alongside this iconic teatime course. The following guide offers recommendations of teas to pair with the various flavor profiles of many recipes in this book, but it should by no means be considered definitive:

AUTUMN SPICES Nepal Ilam Black Tea, Assam Belseri Black Tea, Nilgiri Frost Black Tea

BERRIES Jasmine Green Tea, Darjeeling 1st Flush Black Tea, China Milk Oolong Tea

CARAMEL Golden Monkey Black Tea, Ceylon Kenilworth Estate Black Tea, Kenya Black Tea

CHEESE Assam Golden Tips Black Tea, Bohea Black Tea, Gunpowder Green Tea

CHOCOLATE Keemun Spring Mao Feng Black Tea, most fruit-flavored black teas

CITRUS Darjeeling Ambootia Black Tea, Fujian Ti Kuan Yin Oolong Tea, Earl Grey Black Tea

HERBS Ceylon Lover's Leap Estate Black Tea, Dragonwell Green Tea, Sencha Green Tea

NUTS Nepal Mist Valley Black Tea, Da Hong Pao Oolong Tea, most spice-flavored black teas

OTHER FRUITS Fancy Formosa Oolong Tea, Yunnan Golden Tips Black Tea

TOMATO Winey Keemun Black Tea, Genmaicha Green Tea, Gyokuro Green Tea

TROPICAL FRUITS Jade Oolong Tea, Luan Guapian Green Tea, Oriental Beauty Oolong Tea

VANILLA/PLAIN Cream Earl Grey Black Tea, Taiwanese Gui Fei Oolong Tea, fruity tisanes

A prudent host will prepare the chosen tea in advance of the event to verify that the pairing is pleasing and to determine the most beneficial water temperature and steep time. This will ensure good tea and a delightful teatime. For a list of purveyors of fine teas such as these, turn to page 132.

Plain SCONES

Basic scones are staples of a tearoom's kitchen. These types of scones do not feature fruit, nuts, or savory additions. Instead, they are unadorned and often only slightly seasoned. Since there is no competing flavor, plain scones are perfect vehicles for showcasing a special spread, such as a favorite jam or an unusual curd. In turn, a simple scone is ideal for pairing with a strong-tasting tea, like a flowery Dragon Pearl Jasmine Tea or a fruity Tropical Green Tea. A cream tea, which solely includes tea, scones, and spreads, provides an opportune time to serve a plain scone to highlight the tea and spreads. Whether plain, savory, or sweet, scones are both a welcome necessity and a delightful indulgence at teatime.

SOUR CREAM SCONES
(recipe on page 16)

> *"A Proper Tea is much nicer than a Very Nearly Tea, which is one you forget about afterwards."*
>
> — A.A. Milne

Vanilla Scones
Yield: 12

2 cups self-rising flour
⅓ cup sugar
6 tablespoons cold unsalted butter, cut into pieces
⅓ cup whole buttermilk
¼ cup cold heavy whipping cream
1 large egg
1 tablespoon vanilla extract
1 vanilla bean, split and scraped, seeds reserved
1 egg white, lightly beaten
2 tablespoons vanilla-flavored sugar*

• Preheat oven to 400°.
• Line 2 baking sheets with parchment paper.
• In a large bowl, combine flour and sugar, whisking well. Using a pastry blender, cut butter into flour mixture until mixture resembles coarse crumbs.
• In a medium bowl, combine buttermilk, cream, egg, vanilla extract, and reserved vanilla-bean seeds. Add to flour mixture, stirring until mixture is evenly moist. (Dough will be sticky. If dough seems dry, add more cream, 1 tablespoon at a time.)
• Cut dough in half.
• On a lightly floured surface, roll half of dough into a 6½-inch circle. Cut into 6 wedges. Repeat process with remaining dough. Place scones 2 inches apart on prepared baking sheets.
• Brush scones with egg white, and sprinkle with vanilla-flavored sugar.
• Bake until scones are lightly browned, 9 to 11 minutes.
• Serve warm.

To make vanilla-flavored sugar, place 1 vanilla bean in a resealable plastic bag, along with desired amount of sugar. Seal bag, and let sit until sugar has absorbed vanilla flavor, approximately 24 hours.

Sour Cream Scones
Yield: 9

2 cups all-purpose flour
¼ cup sugar
2 teaspoons baking powder
1 teaspoon fresh lemon zest
½ teaspoon salt
¼ teaspoon baking soda
4 tablespoons cold salted butter, cut into pieces
½ cup sour cream
¼ cup cold heavy whipping cream

• Preheat oven to 400°.
• Line a baking sheet with parchment paper.
• In a large bowl, combine flour, sugar, baking powder, lemon zest, salt, and baking soda, whisking well. Using a pastry blender, cut butter into flour mixture until mixture resembles coarse crumbs.
• In a small bowl, combine sour cream and whipping cream, whisking to blend. Add to flour mixture, stirring until mixture is evenly moist. (If mixture seems dry, add more cream, 1 tablespoon at a time.) Bring mixture together with hands until a dough forms.
• Turn dough out onto a lightly floured surface. Knead gently 4 to 5 times. Using a rolling pin, roll dough to a 1-inch thickness. Using a 2-inch square cutter, cut 9 scones, rerolling scraps as necessary. Place scones 2 inches apart on prepared baking sheet.
• Bake until scones are lightly browned, 10 to 12 minutes.
• Serve warm.

Tea-Upon-Chatsworth
a grandmother's legacy

Many people cherish childhood memories of time spent with their grandparents. But for Elizabeth Savage, the owner of Tea-Upon-Chatsworth in San Diego, California, that time inspired an important career decision.

"I was raised by my Irish grandmother," Elizabeth explains. "We would spend summers in Great Britain, visiting relatives. We used to pop in to countryside tearooms all the time." So when the original owner of Tea-Upon-Chatsworth decided to sell, Elizabeth gave up her career in the financial services industry and bought the tearoom in September 2012.

Elizabeth's goal was to create the type of British tearoom she remembered from her childhood. Armed with her grandmother's recipes, she set out to revise the menu. Her basic scone recipe is based on her grandmother's buttermilk scones. And many other Tea-Upon-Chatsworth favorites, such as her Shepherd's Pie, are scaled-down versions of family recipes.

Like most Americans, Elizabeth grew up drinking black tea. "Once I started traveling for work internationally, I was exposed to a lot of different teas," she says. "I wanted to bring that variety to the tearoom." Her menu now includes 65 teas—from the customer-favorite white açai berry to green teas, oolongs, and black teas. Customers may order as many different ones as they like with afternoon tea.

"It's been great to connect with so many people from around the world—South Africa, Australia, and, of course, Great Britain," Elizabeth says. When newcomers to the tearoom tell her they don't like tea, she replies that they haven't had good tea. "Tea is a much better social drink than coffee or beer or wine. It has great health benefits. It's something you can drink all day long."

Buttermilk Scones
Yield: 18

4½ cups all-purpose flour
½ cup granulated sugar
1 tablespoon plus ¾ teaspoon baking powder
¾ teaspoon baking soda
1½ teaspoons salt
1½ cups cold salted butter, cut into pieces
1½ cups whole buttermilk
1 cup confectioners' sugar
¼ cup boiling water
Garnish: additional confectioners' sugar

- Preheat oven to 350°.
- Line several baking sheets with parchment paper.
- In a large bowl, combine flour, granulated sugar, baking powder, baking soda, and salt, whisking well. Using a pastry blender, cut butter into flour mixture until chunks of butter form small balls about the size of blueberries. Using your hands, break apart balls of butter by sliding your hands back and forth until the mixture looks like fine bread crumbs, being careful not to overhandle.
- Make a hole in the middle of mixture. Add buttermilk to the hole, and fold into mixture by hand without stirring. Continue folding until mixture forms a large ball.
- Turn out dough onto a floured surface, and divide dough into 3 portions.
- Gently shape each portion into a 1-inch-thick round. Cut each into 6 wedges. Place scones 2 inches apart on prepared baking sheets.
- Bake until scones are golden brown, 20 to 30 minutes. Let cool.
- In a medium bowl, combine confectioners' sugar and boiling water, whisking well. Brush glaze onto cooled scones.
- Garnish scones with a sprinkle of additional confectioners' sugar, if desired.

Tea-Upon-Chatsworth | *2180 Chatsworth Boulevard, Suite B • San Diego, CA 92107* | *619-858-2848* | *teauponchatsworth.com*

Sweet SCONES

A bite of a fruit-filled scone topped with a spoonful of Devonshire cream is true bliss. Sweet scones can be enjoyed anytime of day. Alongside a favorite cup of tea, they are an indulgent breakfast. As part of an afternoon-tea menu, sweet scones are decidedly appropriate. And even for a late-night dessert, they can be most welcome. Some recipes feature only one primary flavor addition, while others include a number of tasty items, such as white chocolate and peppermint. One's imagination is the only limit when putting together delicious combinations or presentations. Bring interest to individual plates with sliced-fruit garnishes; top scones with orange curls or fresh herbs; or include fresh, edible flowers. Creativity is always a must when planning a memorable tea.

ORANGE CREAM SCONES
(recipe on page 23)

Editor's Note: See how-to on page 129, or go to teatime magazine.com *to view a step-by-step video of this recipe.*

Blueberry Tea Scones
Yield: 12

1 cup plus 5 tablespoons heavy whipping cream, divided
3 tablespoons blueberry-flavored green tea leaves (from approximately 15 tea bags)
2½ cups all-purpose flour
8 tablespoons sugar, divided
2 teaspoons baking powder
¼ teaspoon salt
⅓ cup cold unsalted butter, cut into pieces
1 large egg, at room temperature
½ cup fresh blueberries
3 tablespoons almond slices
2 tablespoons unsalted butter, melted

• In a small saucepan, heat 1 cup cream over medium heat until just simmering. Remove from heat, add tea leaves, and steep for 10 minutes. Strain, discarding tea leaves. Add enough remaining cream to make 1 cup. Refrigerate until cold, approximately 1 hour.
• Preheat oven to 425°.
• Line a baking sheet with parchment paper.
• In a large bowl, combine flour, 6 tablespoons sugar, baking powder, and salt, whisking well. Using a pastry blender, cut butter into flour mixture until mixture resembles coarse crumbs.
• In a small bowl, combine infused cream and egg, whisking well. Add to flour mixture, stirring until mixture is evenly moist. (If mixture seems dry, add more cream, 1 tablespoon at a time.) Working gently, bring mixture together with hands until a dough forms.
• Turn out dough onto a lightly floured surface, and knead gently several times until smooth. Roll dough to a ½-inch thickness. Using a 2-inch flower-shaped cutter, cut 12 scones, rerolling dough once if needed. Place scones 2 inches apart on prepared baking sheet.
• Brush tops of scones with remaining 5 tablespoons cream. Place 3 or 4 blueberries in the center of each scone. Sprinkle scones with remaining 2 tablespoons sugar. Arrange almond slices as petals on scones.
• Bake until bottom edges of scones are golden brown, 12 to 15 minutes.
• Transfer to a wire rack, and let cool completely. Just before serving, brush with melted butter.

Editor's Note: Please plan ahead. This recipe requires refrigeration.

Blueberry Scones
Yield: 12

2 cups all-purpose flour
⅓ cup sugar
2 teaspoons baking powder
½ teaspoon salt
8 tablespoons cold salted butter, cut into pieces
¾ cup cold heavy whipping cream
1 teaspoon vanilla extract
¼ teaspoon lemon extract
½ cup fresh blueberries

• Preheat oven to 350°.
• Line a baking sheet with parchment paper.
• In large bowl, combine flour, sugar, baking powder, and salt, whisking well. Using a pastry blender, cut butter into flour mixture until mixture resembles coarse crumbs.
• In a liquid-measuring cup, combine cream, vanilla extract, and lemon extract, stirring well. Add to flour mixture, stirring until mixture is evenly moist. (If mixture seems dry, add more cream, 1 tablespoon at a time.) Working gently, bring mixture together with hands until a dough forms.
• Turn dough out onto a lightly floured surface. Knead gently 3 to 4 times. Roll dough to a ½-inch thickness. Scatter ¼ cup blueberries over half of dough. Fold other half of dough over blueberries to enclose them. Lightly roll out dough again to a ½-inch thickness. Repeat scattering, folding, and rolling process with remaining ¼ cup blueberries.
• Using a 2-inch round cutter, cut 12 scones from dough, rerolling scraps as needed. Place scones 2 inches apart on prepared baking sheet.
• Bake until scones are lightly browned, 22 to 24 minutes.
• Serve warm.

Editor's Note: See how-to on page 126, or go to teatimemagazine.com *to view a step-by-step video of this recipe.*

Apricot Cream Scones
Yield: 16

2 cups all-purpose flour
¼ cup sugar
2½ teaspoons baking powder
¼ teaspoon salt
⅓ cup chopped dried apricots
4 tablespoons cold salted butter, cut into pieces
½ cup plus 4 tablespoons cold heavy whipping cream, divided
½ teaspoon vanilla extract

• Preheat oven to 350°.
• Line a rimmed baking sheet with parchment paper.
• In a large bowl, combine flour, sugar, baking powder, and salt, whisking well. Using a pastry blender, cut butter into flour mixture until mixture resembles coarse crumbs. Add dried apricots, stirring to incorporate.
• In a liquid-measuring cup, combine ½ cup plus 3 tablespoons cream and vanilla extract, stirring to blend. Add to flour mixture, stirring until mixture is evenly moist. (If mixture seems dry, add more cream, 1 tablespoon at a time.) Working gently, bring mixture together with hands until a dough forms.
• Turn out dough onto a lightly floured surface, and knead gently 4 to 5 times. Using a rolling pin, roll dough to a ¾-inch thickness. Using a 1¾-inch fluted round cutter, cut 16 scones from dough, rerolling scraps as needed. Place scones 2 inches apart on prepared baking sheet.
• Brush tops of scones with remaining 1 tablespoon cream.
• Bake until edges of scones are golden and a wooden pick inserted in the centers comes out clean, approximately 16 minutes.
• Serve warm.

Caramel and Peach Scones
Yield: 17

2½ cups all-purpose flour
½ cup firmly packed light brown sugar
2 teaspoons baking powder
½ teaspoon salt
8 tablespoons cold unsalted butter, cut into pieces
1 (3-ounce) package cream cheese, cut into small cubes
1 cup finely chopped dried peaches
½ cup caramel bits*
⅔ cup cold heavy whipping cream
1 teaspoon vanilla extract

• Preheat oven to 375°.
• Line a baking sheet with parchment paper.
• In a large bowl, combine flour, brown sugar, baking powder, and salt, whisking well. Using a pastry blender, cut butter into flour mixture until mixture resembles coarse crumbs. Add cream cheese, peaches, and caramel bits, stirring until well combined.
• In a liquid-measuring cup, combine cream and vanilla extract, stirring well. Add to flour mixture, stirring until mixture is evenly moist. (If mixture seems dry, add more cream, 1 tablespoon at a time.) Working gently, bring mixture together with hands until a dough forms.
• Turn out dough onto a lightly floured surface. Roll dough to a ¾-inch thickness. Using a 2-inch square cutter, cut 17 scones, rerolling scraps as needed. Place scones 2 inches apart on prepared baking sheet.
• Bake until scones are lightly browned, 12 to 14 minutes.
• Serve warm.

We used Kraft Caramel Bits.

The McCray House
Tea Room and Gift Shop
a place with character

When Jack and Diane McCray decided to retire, Jack, an avid golfer, had just one request: He wanted to live on the links. Diane agreed, and the two moved from Ohio to McCormick, South Carolina.

While Jack headed for the golf course, Diane was not content to rock on the front porch: She quickly decided to open a tearoom. Diane combed the countryside to find just the right place. "I wanted something with character," she recalls. She discovered a farmhouse that had been vacant for years, and after some remodeling, the McCray House Tea Room and Gift Shop was born.

Charm abounds at McCray House, with its white picket fence surrounding the property. Patrons enter the tearoom via the quintessential front porch. Inside, the main dining room and the "blue room" boast Huguenot-era rafters above the ceiling, gleaming wood floors, and large windows.

Diane rises early to stir and mix because every dish is homemade. She serves two kinds of soups and two kinds of quiches. There is usually a special sandwich of the day, as well as delightful choices for salad lovers, whether they prefer greens, fruit, Diane's chicken salad—or a combination of all three. On the sweet side, guests are treated to the pies that have made Diane's tearoom famous. High tea is available by reservation for groups of 12 or more, but anyone may order a cream tea (scones and tea).

After a trip to Great Britain, where Diane found most of the scones she had were cold or day-old, she vowed to always serve the McCray House's scones "hot out of the oven."

Apricot Scones
Yield: 10

2 cups all-purpose flour
⅓ cup plus 1 tablespoon sugar, divided
2 teaspoons baking powder
⅛ teaspoon salt
⅓ cup cold unsalted butter, cut into pieces
½ cup chopped dried apricots
¼ cup finely chopped walnuts
¾ cup plus 2 tablespoons cold heavy whipping cream, divided
1 large egg, beaten
1 teaspoon vanilla extract

• Preheat oven to 375°.
• Line a baking sheet with parchment paper.
• In a large bowl, combine flour, ⅓ cup sugar, baking powder, and salt, whisking well. Using a pastry blender, cut butter into flour mixture until mixture resembles coarse crumbs. Add apricots and walnuts, stirring to combine.
• In a small bowl, combine ¾ cup cream, egg, and vanilla extract, stirring to blend. Add to flour mixture, stirring until mixture is evenly moist. (If mixture seems dry, add more cream, 1 tablespoon at a time.) Working gently, bring mixture together with hands until a dough forms.
• On a lightly floured surface, pat mixture to a ½-inch thickness. Using a 2-inch round cutter, cut 10 scones, rerolling scraps as needed. Place scones 2 inches apart on prepared baking sheet.
• Lightly brush tops of scones with remaining 2 tablespoons cream, and sprinkle lightly with remaining 1 tablespoon sugar.
• Bake until scones are lightly browned, 15 to 17 minutes.
• Serve warm.

> *" … nowhere is the English genius for domesticity more notably evidenced than in this festival of afternoon tea."*
>
> — James Norwood Pratt

Strawberry-Lavender Scones
Yield: 40

1 cup heavy whipping cream, divided
2 teaspoons culinary lavender
2½ cups sifted bread flour
5 tablespoons sugar
1½ tablespoons baking powder
½ teaspoon salt
¼ teaspoon baking soda
6 tablespoons cold unsalted butter, cut into pieces
½ cup chopped fresh strawberries
½ cup finely chopped toasted almond slivers
2½ tablespoons honey

• In a small microwavable bowl, heat ¾ plus 2 tablespoons cup cream on high in a microwave oven for 30-second intervals until cream simmers. Add lavender, and steep for 5 minutes. Strain, discarding solids. Refrigerate until cold, approximately 1 hour.
• Preheat oven to 400°.
• Line 2 baking sheets with parchment paper.
• In a large bowl, combine flour, sugar, baking powder, salt, and baking soda, whisking well. Using a pastry blender, cut butter into flour mixture until mixture resembles coarse crumbs. Add strawberries and almonds, tossing gently to combine.
• In a liquid-measuring cup, combine honey and lavender-infused cream, stirring well. Add to flour mixture, stirring until mixture is evenly moist. (If mixture seems dry, add more cream, 1 tablespoon at a time.) Working gently, bring mixture together with hands until a dough forms.
• Turn out dough onto a lightly floured surface. Roll dough to a ½-inch thickness. Using a 2-inch square cutter, cut 20 scones, rerolling scraps as needed. Cut squares in half diagonally to form triangles. Place triangular scones 2 inches apart on prepared baking sheets.
• Brush tops with remaining 2 tablespoons cream.
• Bake until scones are light golden brown, 9 to 11 minutes.
• Let cool slightly before serving.

Pear Scones
Yield: 20

2¼ cups self-rising flour
⅓ cup plus 2 tablespoons sugar, divided
½ cup unsalted butter, cut into pieces
1 cup chopped dried pears
⅓ cup whole buttermilk
¼ cup heavy whipping cream
1 large egg, lightly beaten
½ teaspoon vanilla extract
1 large egg white, lightly beaten

• Preheat oven to 400°.
• Line 2 baking sheets with parchment paper.
• In a large bowl, combine flour and ⅓ cup sugar. Using a pastry blender, cut butter into flour mixture until mixture resembles coarse crumbs. Add dried pears, stirring well.
• In a separate bowl, combine buttermilk, cream, egg, and vanilla extract, whisking well. Add to flour mixture, stirring until mixture is evenly moist. (Dough will be sticky. If mixture seems dry, add more cream, 1 tablespoon at a time.)
• On a lightly floured surface, roll dough to a ½-inch thickness. Using a 2¼-inch fluted round cutter, cut 20 scones. Place scones 2 inches apart on prepared baking sheets.
• Brush scones lightly with egg white. Sprinkle evenly with remaining 2 tablespoons sugar.
• Bake until lightly browned, 10 to 12 minutes.

Burdett's Tea Shop
& Trading Company
local favorite

Established in 2001, Burdett's Tea Shop & Trading Company is housed in a circa-1912 building (originally a general store) in the tree-lined historic downtown of Springfield, Tennessee. When owners Sandy and Sam Ramsey bought the building in 2000, their vision was to renovate it but to keep specific original architectural details intact, such as the tin ceiling in what is now the tea shop's dining room.

Burdett's Tea Shop (Burdett is Sandy's maiden name) has dark-paneled walls, a pine floor, and a wonderfully quaint atmosphere. The menu includes Tea Plates, but it also lists a variety of sandwiches, salads, scones, and soups. The chicken salad is a favorite among guests. And there is always a Scone of the Day, featuring such flavors as apricot almond, apple cinnamon, orange cream, and double-chocolate pecan. "We make our scones fresh every day," Sandy says.

Burdett's also has a gift shop that sells serving pieces, aprons, and jewelry, as well as teapots from England, Poland, Russia, and China and even Brown Betty teapots from Staffordshire, England. A new addition to the gift shop is the line of Blue Rose Tea teas, blended by Sandy's daughter, Erin Binkley. Longtime fans of Burdett's Tea Shop needn't worry that their favorite teas, including the wildly popular Russian Caravan, have disappeared from the shop, however. Erin purchased the tea company (including its recipe book) from the previous owner, Hilly Wyne-Smith, who had decided to retire.

"We're very proud of our tea," Sandy says. "We think we can compete with just about anyone."

Orange Cream Scones
Yield: 12

3 cups all-purpose flour
½ cup sugar
2½ teaspoons baking powder
1 teaspoon salt
½ teaspoon baking soda
¾ cup unsalted butter, cut into pieces
1 cup whole buttermilk
1 tablespoon fresh orange zest
1 tablespoon frozen orange juice concentrate
1 teaspoon vanilla extract
¼ cup heavy whipping cream
1 recipe Powdered Sugar Glaze (recipe follows)

• Preheat oven to 450°.
• Line a baking sheet with parchment paper.
• In a large bowl, combine flour, sugar, baking powder, salt, and baking soda, whisking well. Using a pastry blender, cut butter into flour mixture until mixture resembles coarse crumbs.
• In a small bowl, combine buttermilk, orange zest, orange juice concentrate, and vanilla extract, stirring until blended. Add to flour mixture, stirring until mixture is evenly moist. (If mixture seems dry, add more buttermilk, 1 tablespoon at a time.) Working gently, bring mixture together with hands until a dough forms. Do not overwork dough.
• Turn out dough onto a lightly floured surface. Work into a mound, kneading lightly. Roll into a ½-inch-thick circle. Cut dough into 12 wedges. Place scones 2 inches apart on prepared baking sheet.
• Brush tops of scones with cream.
• Bake for 9 minutes. Turn pan around, and bake until scones are lightly browned, 3 to 5 minutes.
• Let cool slightly. Drizzle with Powdered Sugar Glaze.

Powdered Sugar Glaze
Yield: ¾ cup

2 cups confectioners' sugar
1 to 2 tablespoons warm water

• In a bowl, combine confectioners' sugar and 1 tablespoon water, stirring well. Add remaining 1 tablespoon water as needed to achieve a good consistency for drizzling, being careful not to get glaze too thin.

Key Lime Scones

Yield: 12

2 cups all-purpose flour
⅓ cup plus 1 teaspoon sugar, divided
3 tablespoons fresh Key lime zest*
2½ teaspoons baking powder
½ teaspoon salt
4 tablespoons cold salted butter, cut into pieces
1 (3-ounce) package cream cheese, cut into small cubes
½ cup plus 1 tablespoon cold heavy whipping cream, divided
1 large egg, lightly beaten
1½ tablespoons fresh Key lime juice*
1 teaspoon vanilla extract
1 recipe Ginger Curd (recipe on page 119)

• Preheat oven to 350°.
• Line a baking sheet with parchment paper.
• In a medium bowl, combine flour, ⅓ cup sugar, lime zest, baking powder, and salt, whisking well. Using a pastry blender, cut butter and cream cheese into flour mixture until mixture resembles coarse crumbs.
• In a liquid-measuring cup, combine ½ cup cream, egg, lime juice, and vanilla extract, stirring well. Add to flour mixture, stirring until mixture is evenly moist. (If mixture seems dry, add more cream, 1 tablespoon at a time.) Working gently, bring mixture together with hands until a dough forms.
• Turn out dough onto a lightly floured surface, and knead gently 4 to 5 times. Roll dough to a ¾-inch thickness. Using a 2-inch fluted round cutter, cut 12 scones, rerolling scraps as needed. Place scones 2 inches apart on prepared baking sheet.
• Using a pastry brush, lightly brush tops of scones with remaining 1 tablespoon cream. Evenly sprinkle with remaining 1 teaspoon sugar.
• Bake until scones are lightly browned, 18 to 20 minutes.
• Serve warm with Ginger Curd, if desired.

If Key limes are not available, you may substitute regular limes.

Orange Cream Scones

Yield: 12

2½ cups all-purpose flour
½ cup plus 2 tablespoons sugar, divided
2 teaspoons baking powder
½ teaspoon salt
8 tablespoons cold salted butter, cut into pieces
1 tablespoon fresh orange zest

⅔ cup plus 1 tablespoon cold heavy whipping cream, divided
½ teaspoon orange extract
1 recipe Strawberry Curd (recipe on page 119)

• Preheat oven to 375°.
• Line a baking sheet with parchment paper.
• In a large bowl, combine flour, ½ cup sugar, baking powder, and salt, whisking well. Using a pastry blender, cut butter into flour mixture until mixture resembles coarse crumbs. Add orange zest, stirring well.
• In a liquid-measuring cup, combine ⅔ cup cream and orange extract. Add to flour mixture, stirring until mixture is evenly moist. (If mixture seems dry, add more cream, 1 tablespoon at a time.) Working gently, bring mixture together with hands until a dough forms.
• On a lightly floured surface, roll dough to a ½-inch thickness. Using a 2¼-inch fluted round cutter, cut 12 scones, rerolling scraps as needed. Place scones 2 inches apart on prepared baking sheet.
• Brush scones with remaining 1 tablespoon cream, and sprinkle with remaining 2 tablespoons sugar.
• Bake until scones are lightly browned, 18 to 20 minutes.
• Serve with Strawberry Curd, if desired.

- Cut dough in half.
- On a lightly floured surface, roll half of dough into a 6½-inch circle. Cut into 6 wedges. Repeat process with remaining dough. Place scones 2 inches apart on prepared baking sheets.
- In a small bowl, lightly beat remaining egg. Brush scones with beaten egg, and sprinkle with remaining 2 tablespoons sugar.
- Bake until scones are lightly browned, 12 to 14 minutes.
- Serve warm.

Orange-Currant Scones
Yield: 12 to 16

¾ cup whole milk
2 teaspoons fresh lemon juice
2 cups all-purpose flour
3 tablespoons sugar
1 tablespoon baking powder
½ teaspoon salt
3 tablespoons cold unsalted butter, cut into pieces
½ cup dried currants
1 teaspoon fresh orange zest
1 large egg, lightly beaten
3 tablespoons heavy whipping cream

- Preheat oven to 450°.
- Stack 2 baking sheets together, and line the top pan with parchment paper. (This prevents overbrowning.)
- In a small bowl, combine milk and lemon juice. Set aside for 10 minutes to let milk curdle.
- In a large bowl, combine flour, sugar, baking powder, and salt, whisking well. Using a pastry blender, cut butter into flour mixture until mixture resembles coarse crumbs. Add currants and orange zest, tossing to combine.
- Add milk mixture and egg to flour mixture, stirring until mixture is evenly moist. (If mixture seems dry, add more milk, 1 tablespoon at a time.) Working gently, bring mixture together with hands until a dough forms.
- Turn out dough onto a floured surface, and knead gently 4 or 5 times. Pat or roll dough to a ½-inch thickness. Using a 2-inch fluted round cutter, cut as many scones as possible, rerolling dough as needed. Place scones 2 inches apart on prepared baking sheet.
- Brush tops of scones with cream.
- Bake until edges of scones are lightly brown, 10 to 12 minutes.
- Serve warm.

Orange-Fig Scones
Yield: 12

2 cups all-purpose flour
¼ cup plus 2 tablespoons sugar, divided
1½ teaspoons baking powder
½ teaspoon salt
6 tablespoons cold salted butter, cut into pieces
⅔ cup chopped dried figs
2 tablespoons fresh orange zest
½ cup cold heavy whipping cream
2 large eggs, divided
1 teaspoon vanilla extract

- Preheat oven to 400°.
- Line 2 baking sheets with parchment paper.
- In a large bowl, combine flour, ¼ cup sugar, baking powder, and salt, whisking well. Using a pastry blender, cut butter into flour mixture until mixture resembles coarse crumbs. Add figs and orange zest, stirring well.
- In a liquid-measuring cup, combine cream, 1 egg, and vanilla extract, stirring well. Add to flour mixture, stirring until mixture is evenly moist. (Mixture will be sticky. If it seems dry, add more cream, 1 tablespoon at a time.) Working gently, bring mixture together with hands until a dough forms.

Laura's Tea Room
mother-and-daughter duo

When Carol Allen opened Laura's Tea Room eight years ago, she knew she had found the perfect place for a tearoom—a 105-year-old mercantile building in historic Ridgeway, South Carolina, with original heart-pine floors. In a café on the first floor, guests can order a pot of loose-leaf tea with sandwiches, soups, and salads. But those in search of traditional afternoon tea must climb the steps to the third floor where that elegant meal is served with all the flourishes.

Afternoon tea consists of two to four courses (the menu changes monthly), beginning with scones served with homemade Devon cream and lemon curd. Carol's mother, Eleanor, who just celebrated her 95th birthday, makes 300 scones for the tearoom each weekend and also makes the lemon curd from scratch. Guests enjoy a savory course of quiche or soup, along with a green salad, followed by a three-tiered tray with treats such as cucumber sandwiches, strawberries and cream cheese, and more.

"We never reset a table," Carol says. "When all of our tables are taken, we're full for the day." Guests are allowed to linger over tea for two hours or more, however, if they like. "We just keep bringing pots of tea."

Carol has witnessed friendships being made and relationships being rekindled there. She recalls a mother and a daughter (age 18 or 19), who began coming to the tearoom monthly when it first opened. "In the beginning, there was no conversation at their table. They just sat there quietly not speaking to each other," she says. But each month, they would talk a little more, and after one year, the change was amazing. "They told me that taking tea together had saved their relationship."

"There are so many reasons for taking tea," Carol concludes.

Orange-Pecan Scones
Yield: 16

2 cups self-rising flour
½ cup granulated sugar
1 teaspoon fresh orange zest
⅓ cup cold unsalted butter, cut into pieces
½ cup whole buttermilk
¼ cup fresh orange juice
⅓ cup chopped pecans
1 teaspoon vanilla extract
2 tablespoons castor sugar
1 recipe Laura's Tea Room's Devonshire Cream
  (recipe on page 124)

• Preheat oven to 425°.
• Spray wells of a scone pan* with baking spray with flour.
• In a large bowl, combine flour, granulated sugar, and orange zest, whisking well. Using a pastry blender, cut butter into flour mixture until mixture resembles coarse crumbs. Add buttermilk, orange juice, pecans, and vanilla extract, stirring just until combined. (If mixture seems dry, add more buttermilk, 1 tablespoon at a time.)
• Divide dough among wells of prepared pan. Shape dough slightly, but do not handle dough too much as this is a very light scone. Sprinkle with castor sugar.
• Bake until scones are lightly browned, 12 to 14 minutes.
• Serve warm with Laura's Tea Room's Devonshire Cream, if desired.

We used a Nordicware Mini Scone Pan with 16 wedge-shaped wells.

- Using a levered 3-tablespoon scoop, drop dough 2 inches apart onto prepared baking sheets.
- Bake until edges are golden brown and a wooden pick inserted in centers comes out clean, approximately 18 minutes. Remove to a wire rack.
- While scones bake, prepare glaze. In a small bowl, combine confectioners' sugar, remaining 1 teaspoon orange zest, and orange juice, whisking until smooth. Spoon over warm scones.
- Serve warm or at room temperature the same day.

We used White Lily Enriched Bleached Self-Rising Flour, available in grocery stores throughout the Southeastern region of the United States and online at whitelily.com.

†*Before measuring coconut milk, empty contents into a small bowl, and whisk together to combine solids and liquids.*

White Chocolate–Macadamia Nut Drop Scones
Yield: 18 to 20

2 cups all-purpose flour
⅓ cup plus 2 tablespoons sugar, divided
1½ teaspoons baking powder
1 teaspoon baking soda
½ teaspoon salt
6 tablespoons cold unsalted butter, cut into pieces
½ cup white chocolate morsels
½ cup chopped macadamia nuts
⅔ cup whole buttermilk
1 large egg, lightly beaten
1 teaspoon vanilla extract

- Preheat oven to 350°.
- Line 2 baking sheets with parchment paper.
- In a large bowl, combine flour, ⅓ cup sugar, baking powder, baking soda, and salt, whisking well. Using a pastry blender, cut butter into flour mixture until mixture resembles coarse crumbs. Add white chocolate morsels and macadamia nuts, stirring to combine.
- In a liquid-measuring cup, combine buttermilk, egg, and vanilla extract, stirring well. Add to flour mixture, stirring just until combined. (Dough will be sticky. If mixture seems dry, add more buttermilk, 1 tablespoon at a time.) Working gently, bring mixture together with hands until a dough forms.
- Drop dough by heaping teaspoonfuls onto prepared baking sheets.
- Sprinkle scones with remaining 2 tablespoons sugar.
- Bake until scones are lightly browned, 14 to 16 minutes.

Ambrosia Scones
Yield: approximately 16

3 cups self-rising soft-wheat flour*
½ cup granulated sugar
1 tablespoon plus 1 teaspoon fresh orange zest, divided
8 tablespoons cold salted butter, cut into pieces
1 cup coconut milk†
2 teaspoons coconut extract
½ cup confectioners' sugar
2 tablespoons fresh orange juice

- Preheat oven to 350°.
- Line 2 baking sheets with parchment paper.
- In a medium bowl, combine flour, granulated sugar, and 1 tablespoon orange zest, whisking well. Using a pastry blender, cut butter into flour mixture until mixture resembles coarse crumbs.
- In a small bowl, combine coconut milk and coconut extract, whisking well. Add to flour mixture, stirring until a soft dough forms. (If mixture seems dry and dough won't come together, add more coconut milk, 1 tablespoon at a time.)

A Cup of Tea
victorian tearoom in paradise

Darlene Pahed, owner of A Cup of Tea in Kailua, Hawaii, loves all things Victorian. Her home is decorated in a Victorian theme. One day she said to her husband, Jay, "You know, there's no Victorian tearoom in this entire state. I need to open one." With his blessing, she boarded a flight to California, traveling the length of the state to research the best practices for tearooms. Armed with her newfound knowledge, Darlene opened A Cup of Tea in 2007 in the town of Kailua on the west coast of Oahu.

When customers enter A Cup of Tea, it's like stepping into a different world, Darlene says. Beautiful classical music is playing in the background, and the tearoom is charmingly decorated in one of five seasonal themes. Some customers have told Darlene they can even feel their blood pressure dropping. "Our tearoom has a very calming effect on people," she points out.

A Cup of Tea is a Victorian tearoom, Darlene insists. The waitresses wear Victorian-style mop caps and aprons. The portions served at afternoon tea, however, are generous since Hawaiian custom says letting people leave your house hungry will bring shame on your family. If you want more tea sandwiches, just ask your waitress. "We want to make sure that no one leaves hungry," Darlene says.

"Hawaii is a vacation destination, so we get our fair share of tourists from England, Australia, New Zealand, and even Japan," she points out. (Japanese people are fascinated by the English style of taking tea, she confides.) And Darlene has even entertained a celebrity or two. One Sunday, she served tea to Alistair Bruce, the technical advisor for the PBS television series *Downton Abbey*.

In 2008, A Cup of Tea won the prestigious Ilima Award, presented to the best new restaurant in Hawaii. Many prominent people attended the award presentation, and Darlene couldn't resist remarking to Jay, "Imagine that—we serve egg-salad sandwiches!"

Coconut Scones
Yield: 22 to 24 scones

2 cups all-purpose flour
2 tablespoons granulated sugar
1 tablespoon baking powder
½ teaspoon salt
4 tablespoons cold butter,
 cut into pieces
1 cup whole milk
1 cup sweetened flaked coconut
Garnish: confectioners' sugar

• Preheat oven to 325°.
• Spray 2 rimmed baking sheets with nonstick cooking spray.
• In a large bowl, combine flour, granulated sugar, baking powder, and salt, whisking well. Using a pastry blender, cut butter into flour mixture until mixture resembles coarse crumbs. Add milk, stirring well. (Dough will be sticky.) Sprinkle coconut over dough, and fold to combine.
• Using a levered 1½-tablespoon scoop, drop dough 2 inches apart onto prepared baking sheets.
• Bake until scones are lightly browned, 15 to 18 minutes.
• Just before serving, garnish with a dusting of confectioners' sugar, if desired.

- Bake until scones are lightly browned, 20 to 22 minutes.

To achieve the look pictured on the front of the book, drizzle melted chocolate-hazelnut spread, such as Nutella, over each wedge.

Editor's Note: Go to teatimemagazine.com to view a step-by-step video of this recipe.

Cherry-Rose Scones
Yield: 24

2½ cups all-purpose flour
½ cup plus 2 tablespoons sugar, divided
2 teaspoons baking powder
½ teaspoon salt
8 tablespoons cold unsalted butter, cut into pieces
1 (3-ounce) package cold cream cheese, cut into pieces
1 (2-ounce) package dehydrated cherries*, finely chopped
⅓ cup cold heavy whipping cream
1 teaspoon rose water†
½ teaspoon vanilla extract
¼ teaspoon cherry extract

- Preheat oven to 375°.
- Line 2 baking sheets with parchment paper.
- In a large bowl, combine flour, ½ cup sugar, baking powder, and salt, whisking well. Using a pastry blender, cut butter and cream cheese into flour mixture until mixture resembles coarse crumbs. Add cherries, stirring to combine.
- In a liquid-measuring cup, combine cream, rose water, vanilla extract, and cherry extract, stirring well. Add to flour mixture, stirring until mixture is evenly moist. (If mixture seems dry, add more cream, 1 tablespoon at a time.) Working gently, bring mixture together with hands until a dough forms.
- On a lightly floured surface, roll dough to a ¾-inch thickness. Using a 2-inch round cutter, cut 24 scones, rerolling scraps as needed. Place scones 2 inches apart on prepared baking sheets.
- Sprinkle scones evenly with remaining 2 tablespoons sugar.
- Bake until scones are light golden brown, 13 to 15 minutes.
- Serve warm.

We used Organic Just Cherries, which can be purchased at specialty-foods stores or at justtomatoes.com.

†*Rose water can be purchased at Middle Eastern markets, specialty-foods stores, or at americanspice.com.*

Hazelnut Wedge Scones
Yield: 12 to 16

2½ cups all-purpose flour
⅓ cup granulated sugar
2½ teaspoons baking powder
¼ teaspoon salt
8 tablespoons cold salted butter, cut into pieces
¼ cup finely grated bittersweet chocolate
½ cup toasted chopped hazelnuts
¾ cup cold heavy whipping cream
1 large egg
1 large egg white, lightly beaten
Garnish: castor sugar

- Preheat oven to 350°.
- Line 2 baking sheets with parchment paper.
- In a large bowl, combine flour, granulated sugar, baking powder, and salt, whisking well. Using a pastry blender, cut butter into flour mixture until mixture resembles coarse crumbs. Add chocolate and hazelnuts, stirring to combine.
- In a liquid-measuring cup, combine cream and egg, whisking well. Add to flour mixture, stirring until mixture is evenly moist. (If mixture seems dry, add more cream, 1 tablespoon at a time.) Working gently, bring mixture together with hands until a dough forms.
- Cut dough in half.
- On a lightly floured surface, roll half of dough into a 7-inch circle. Cut into 6 or 8 wedges. Repeat process with remaining dough. Place scones 2 inches apart on prepared baking sheets.
- Brush dough with lightly beaten egg white, and sprinkle with castor sugar, if desired.

*If honey-flavored rooibos is not available, use honeybush or unflavored rooibos. Rooibos and honeybush are native to South Africa and are not considered real tea because they do not come from the Camellia sinensis plant.

Rooibos-Infused Cherry Scones
Yield: 16

⅔ cup whole milk
1 (.05-ounce) bag honey-flavored rooibos
(approximately 1 teaspoon loose rooibos)*
2 teaspoons fresh lemon juice
2 cups all-purpose flour
¼ cup sugar
1 teaspoon baking powder
¼ teaspoon baking soda
¼ teaspoon salt
8 tablespoons cold unsalted butter, cut into pieces
¼ cup chopped dried cherries
2 tablespoons heavy whipping cream

• In a small saucepan, bring milk to a simmer over medium heat. Remove from heat, and place rooibos bag in milk. Steep for 10 minutes. Remove bag, and let milk cool to room temperature, approximately 20 minutes.
• Add lemon juice to milk, stirring to combine. Set aside for 10 minutes to let milk curdle.
• Preheat oven to 400°.
• Line 2 baking sheets with parchment paper.
• In a large bowl, combine flour, sugar, baking powder, baking soda, and salt, whisking well. Using a pastry blender, cut butter into flour mixture until mixture resembles coarse crumbs. Add cherries, stirring to combine.
• Gradually add curdled tea-infused milk, stirring until mixture is evenly moist. (If mixture seems dry, add more milk, 1 tablespoon at a time.) Working gently, bring mixture together with hands until a dough forms.
• Turn out dough onto a lightly floured surface, and knead gently 6 to 10 times.
• Cut dough in half. Roll each half of dough into a ½-inch-thick circle. Cut each circle into 8 wedges. Place scones 2 inches apart on prepared baking sheets.
• Brush scones with cream.
• Bake until scones are light golden brown, 10 to 15 minutes.
• Serve warm.

Fig and Honey Scones
Yield: 19

2½ cups sifted bread flour
3 tablespoons sugar
1½ tablespoons baking powder
½ teaspoon salt
6 tablespoons cold unsalted butter, cut into pieces
½ cup chopped dried figs
½ cup finely chopped toasted walnuts
2½ tablespoons honey
1 cup plus 3 tablespoons cold heavy whipping cream, divided

• Preheat oven to 400°.
• Line a baking sheet with parchment paper.
• In a large bowl, combine flour, sugar, baking powder, and salt, whisking well. Using a pastry blender, cut butter into flour mixture until mixture resembles coarse crumbs. Add figs and walnuts, tossing gently to combine.
• In a liquid-measuring cup, combine 1 cup plus 2 tablespoons cream and honey, stirring to blend. Add to flour mixture, stirring until mixture is evenly moist. (If mixture seems dry, add more cream, 1 tablespoon at a time.) Working gently, bring mixture together with hands until a dough forms.
• Turn out dough onto a lightly floured surface, and knead gently 4 to 5 times. Roll dough to a ½-inch thickness. Using a 2-inch square cutter, cut 19 scones, rerolling scraps as needed. Place scones 2 inches apart on prepared baking sheet.
• Brush tops of scones with remaining 1 tablespoon cream.
• Bake until scones are light golden brown, 10 to 12 minutes.
• Serve warm.

Thyme-out Tea Parties
the traveling tea party

Many tearoom owners got their start by hosting in-home tea parties. But Susan Asher, the owner of Thyme-out Tea Parties in Quincy, Illinois, turned that business model upside down. "I had a brief thought of getting started having tea parties and someday opening a brick-and-mortar tearoom," she recalls. "But that lasted about three weeks." The military veteran with more than 20 years of service realized she didn't want to be a full-time tearoom owner. "I wanted a little more freedom and flexibility with my schedule," Susan says.

The solution was Susan's traveling afternoon-tea company, Thyme-out Tea Parties, where she has been taking tea on the road for more than 14 years. As part of her services, Susan creates beautiful English-style teatimes in her customers' homes, providing table settings, linen napkins, background music, and centerpieces for the event. She also prepares and serves the food on location, with the typical menu including scones, three types of tea sandwiches, desserts, and two teas (one decaffeinated or one herbal).

Susan developed her recipe for White Chocolate–Cherry Scones during the early days of her business. Occasionally, she replaces the dried cherries with dried apples or fresh strawberries and blueberries. Her Lemon Curd Whipped Topping (page 124) is a recipe she came up with after experimenting with homemade whipped cream and several curds and fruit butters.

"There's always a good excuse for a tea party," Susan points out. She has hosted bridal showers, baby showers, and birthday parties in her customers' homes. She became so good at planning tea parties (it's the military training, she says) that it led to her second business—teaching other people how to start their own tea-party businesses.

White Chocolate–Cherry Scones
Yield: 12

2 cups all-purpose flour
5 tablespoons sugar, divided
2½ teaspoons baking powder
¼ teaspoon baking soda
2 tablespoons fresh orange zest
½ cup cold salted butter, cut into pieces
½ cup dried cherries
½ cup white chocolate morsels
2 large eggs, divided
½ cup half-and-half
1 teaspoon vanilla extract
1 recipe Thyme-out Tea Parties' Lemon Curd Whipped Topping (recipe on page 124)

• Heat oven to 385°.
• Line a baking sheet with parchment paper.
• In a large bowl, combine flour, 3 tablespoons sugar, baking powder, baking soda, and orange zest, whisking well. Using a pastry blender, cut butter into flour mixture until mixture resembles coarse crumbs. Add cherries and white chocolate morsels, stirring to combine.
• In a small bowl, gently beat 1 egg. Add half-and-half and vanilla extract. Add to flour mixture, stirring until just combined. (If mixture seems dry, add more half-and-half, 1 tablespoon at a time.) Working gently, bring mixture together with hands until a dough forms.
• Turn dough out onto a lightly floured surface, and knead lightly 10 times. Do not overwork dough. Roll into a 9-inch circle, and cut into 12 wedges. Place scones 2 inches apart on prepared baking sheet.
• In another small bowl, beat remaining egg. Brush tops of scones with beaten egg, and sprinkle with remaining 2 tablespoons sugar. Set aside for 15 minutes before baking.
• Bake until scones are golden brown, 14 to 16 minutes.
• Serve warm with Thyme-out Tea Parties' Lemon Curd Whipped Topping, if desired.

Chocolate Chip Scones
Yield: 12

2 cups all-purpose flour
⅓ cup plus 1 teaspoon sugar, divided
2 teaspoons baking powder
½ teaspoon salt
6 tablespoons cold salted butter, cut into pieces
1 cup milk chocolate morsels
¾ cup plus 1 tablespoon cold heavy whipping cream,
    divided
1 large egg yolk
1 teaspoon vanilla extract
1 recipe Strawberry Sweet Cream (recipe on page 115)

• Preheat oven to 350°.
• Line a baking sheet with parchment paper.
• In a large bowl, combine flour, ⅓ cup sugar, baking powder, and salt, whisking well. Using a pastry blender, cut butter into flour mixture until mixture resembles coarse crumbs. Add chocolate morsels, stirring to combine.
• In a liquid-measuring cup, combine ¾ cup cream, egg yolk, and vanilla extract, stirring well. Add to flour mixture, stirring until mixture is evenly moist. (If mixture seems dry, add more cream, 1 tablespoon at a time.) Working gently, bring mixture together with hands until a dough forms.
• On a lightly floured surface, roll dough to a 1-inch thickness. Using a 2¼-inch round cutter, cut 12 scones, rerolling scraps as needed. Place scones 2 inches apart on prepared baking sheet.
• Brush tops of scones evenly with remaining 1 table-spoon cream, and sprinkle with remaining 1 teaspoon sugar.
• Bake until scones are lightly browned, 18 to 20 minutes.
• Serve warm with Strawberry Sweet Cream, if desired.

Chocolate Chip–Cherry Scones
Yield: 12

2½ cups all-purpose flour
½ cup sugar
2 teaspoons baking powder
½ teaspoon salt
8 tablespoons cold unsalted butter, cut into pieces
1 (3-ounce) package cold cream cheese, cut into
    pieces
¾ cup chopped dried cherries
½ cup mini chocolate morsels
⅓ cup cold heavy whipping cream
1 teaspoon almond extract
½ cup sliced almonds

• Preheat oven to 375°.
• Line a baking sheet with parchment paper.
• In a large bowl, combine flour, sugar, baking powder, and salt, whisking well. Using a pastry blender, cut butter and cream cheese into flour mixture until mixture resembles coarse crumbs. Add cherries and chocolate morsels, stirring to combine.
• In a liquid-measuring cup, combine cream and almond extract, stirring well. Add to flour mixture, stirring until mixture is evenly moist. (If mixture seems dry, add more cream, 1 tablespoon at a time.) Working gently, bring mixture together with hands until a dough forms.
• On a lightly floured surface, roll dough to a ¾-inch thickness. Using a 2½-inch heart-shaped cutter, cut 12 scones, rerolling scraps as needed. Place scones 2 inches apart on prepared baking sheet.
• Sprinkle scones with sliced almonds.
• Bake until scones are light golden brown, 13 to 15 minutes.
• Serve warm.

Sweet Afton Tea Room & Governor Croswell Tea Room

twice as nice

Instead of traveling the country in an RV, retirement for Phyllis and Al Wilkerson meant chasing their dream of owning a restaurant, a dream realized with the purchase of the Sweet Afton Tea Room in Plymouth, Michigan. Phyllis had for years taken their three daughters to the charming tearoom, and when it became available for purchase, the couple decided it was meant to be.

The Wilkersons later opened the Governor Croswell Tea Room, an hour away in Adrian, Michigan, Al's hometown. The tearoom, named for former Michigan governor Charles M. Croswell, is in the 140-year-old Hoefler Building that boasts a stunning white terra-cotta Beaux-Arts facade, original maple floors, and coffered ceilings.

Each tearoom has its own personality, yet they share the wonderful hospitality and hearty menu that have made each a destination unto itself. Though the names of dishes may vary between the two, guests may dine on such delights as chicken potpie and shepherd's pie. Six different flavors of made-from-scratch scones are on offer daily, all accompanied by homemade lemon curd, Devonshire cream, and strawberry preserves. The selection of desserts is impressive, from the signature Ayrshire Cream to Victorian Sponge Cake, and more. And for fans of high tea, a three-course version is served all day at both tearooms.

Many wonderful occasions are celebrated at the tearooms, and they host a number of special events. For example, Sweet Afton opened at 4 o'clock a.m. so patrons could don their prettiest bonnets to celebrate William and Kate's royal wedding in real time.

The Wilkersons cherish the relationships they have built with their patrons. "We have customers who drive five or six hours just to eat here," says Phyllis. "They've become family— I feel like they are coming into my own dining room."

Chocolate-Cherry Scones
Yield: 19 to 20

3½ cups all purpose flour
¼ cup sugar
2 tablespoons baking powder
6 tablespoons cold salted butter, cut into
  small pieces
1 cup mini semisweet chocolate morsels
¾ cups chopped dried cherries
5 large eggs
⅔ cup whole buttermilk
¼ to ½ cup melted dipping chocolate

• Preheat oven to 350°.
• Line 2 baking sheets with parchment paper.
• In a large bowl, combine flour, sugar, and baking powder, whisking well. Using a pastry blender, cut butter into flour mixture until mixture resembles coarse crumbs. Add chocolate chips and dried cherries, stirring to combine.
• In a 2-cup liquid measuring cup, whisk eggs. Add buttermilk, and whisk again. (Mixture should equal 2 cups; add more buttermilk, if needed.) Add to flour mixture, and mix together until dry ingredients are wet. (Batter should still be lumpy.) Do not overmix.
• Using a levered ¼-cup (#16) scoop, drop dough 2 inches apart onto prepared baking sheets.
• Bake until scones are golden brown, approximately 17 minutes.
• Drizzle scones with melted chocolate.
• Serve warm with strawberry preserves, whipped Devonshire cream, and lemon curd.

Sweet Afton Tea Room | *450 Forest Avenue • Plymouth, MI 48170* | *734-454-0777* | sweetaftontearoom.com
Governor Croswell Tea Room | *125 E. Maumee • Adrian, MI 49221* | *517-759-4249* | governorcroswelltearoom.com

White Chocolate–Peppermint Scones

Yield: 10

2 cups all-purpose flour
¼ cup sugar
2 teaspoons baking powder
½ teaspoon salt
4 tablespoons cold salted butter, cut into pieces
½ cup chopped white chocolate
½ cup crushed soft peppermint candies
¾ cup cold heavy whipping cream
½ teaspoon vanilla extract
½ teaspoon peppermint extract
1 recipe Peppermint Cream (recipe on page 118)

• Preheat oven to 350°.
• Line a baking sheet with parchment paper.
• In a large bowl, combine flour, sugar, baking powder, and salt, whisking well. Using a pastry blender, cut butter into flour mixture until mixture resembles coarse crumbs. Add white chocolate and crushed peppermint, stirring to combine.
• In a liquid-measuring cup, combine cream, vanilla extract, and peppermint extract. Add to flour mixture, stirring until mixture is evenly moist. (If mixture seems dry, add more cream, 1 tablespoon at a time.) Working gently, bring mixture together with hands until a dough forms.
• Turn out dough onto a lightly floured surface, and knead gently 4 to 5 times. Roll dough to a ¾-inch thickness. Using a 2-inch round cutter, cut 10 scones, rerolling scraps as needed. Place scones 2 inches apart on prepared baking sheet.
• Bake until scones are light golden brown, 18 to 20 minutes.
• Serve with Peppermint Cream, if desired.

Red Velvet Scones with Cream Cheese Glaze

Yield: 15

2¼ cups all-purpose flour
⅔ cup sugar
¼ cup natural unsweetened cocoa powder
1 teaspoon baking soda
¼ teaspoon salt
8 tablespoons cold unsalted butter, cut into pieces
¾ cup plus 1 tablespoon cold heavy whipping cream, divided
1 large egg
2 tablespoons red food coloring
½ teaspoon vanilla extract
1 recipe Cream Cheese Glaze (recipe follows)

• Preheat oven to 350°.
• Line 2 baking sheets with parchment paper.
• In a large bowl, combine flour, sugar, cocoa powder, baking soda, and salt, whisking well. Using a pastry blender, cut butter into flour mixture until mixture resembles coarse crumbs.
• In a liquid-measuring cup, combine ¾ cup cream, egg, food coloring, and vanilla extract, whisking well. Add to flour mixture, stirring until mixture is evenly moist. (Dough will be slightly sticky. If mixture seems dry, add more cream, 1 tablespoon at a time.)
• On a lightly floured surface, roll dough to a ½-inch thickness. Using a 2½-inch heart-shaped cutter, cut 15 scones, rerolling dough as needed. Place scones 2 inches apart on prepared baking sheets.
• Brush tops of scones evenly with remaining 1 tablespoon cream.
• Bake until scones are lightly browned, 10 to 12 minutes. Let cool completely on wire racks.
• Drizzle or pipe scones with Cream Cheese Glaze, if desired.

Cream Cheese Glaze

Yield: 1½ cups

1 (3-ounce) package cream cheese, softened
1 cup confectioners' sugar
1 tablespoon heavy whipping cream

• In a mixing bowl, combine cream cheese, confectioners' sugar, and cream. Beat at low speed with a mixer until smooth.

• Bake until scones are light golden brown, 8 to 10 minutes. Let cool on wire racks.
• Place melted chocolate in a small pastry bag fitted with a small round tip. Pipe melted chocolate in a bow design onto scones, if desired.

Salted Caramel Scones
Yield: 12

2½ cups all-purpose flour
½ cup granulated sugar
2 teaspoons baking powder
½ teaspoon salt
12 tablespoons cold unsalted butter, divided
1 (3-ounce) package cream cheese, cut into small cubes
½ cup caramel bits*
½ cup cold heavy whipping cream
1 teaspoon vanilla extract
¼ cup firmly packed light brown sugar
2 tablespoons coarse sea salt
1 recipe Caramel Sauce (recipe on page 118) or prepared caramel topping

• Preheat oven to 375°.
• Line a baking sheet with parchment paper.
• In a large bowl, combine flour, sugar, baking powder, and salt, whisking well. Using a pastry blender, cut 8 tablespoons butter into flour mixture until mixture resembles coarse crumbs. Add cream cheese and caramel bits, stirring until well combined.
• In a liquid-measuring cup, combine cream and vanilla extract, stirring to blend. Add to flour mixture, stirring until mixture is evenly moist. (If mixture seems dry, add more cream, 1 tablespoon at a time.) Working gently, bring mixture together with hands until a dough forms.
• On a lightly floured surface, roll dough to a ¾-inch thickness. Using a 2½-inch round fluted cutter, cut 12 scones, rerolling scraps as needed. Place scones 2 inches apart on prepared baking sheet.
• In a small saucepan, combine brown sugar and remaining 4 tablespoons butter over medium heat. Cook until mixture is smooth, approximately 8 minutes, stirring often. Brush tops of scones with brown sugar mixture, and sprinkle evenly with sea salt.
• Bake until scones are light golden brown, 12 to 14 minutes.
• Garnish with Caramel Sauce, if desired. Serve with additional Caramel Sauce, if desired.

We used Kraft Premium Caramel Bits, which can be found on the baking supplies aisle at most supermarkets.

Caramel Scones
Yield: 16

2 cups all-purpose flour
⅓ cup firmly packed light brown sugar
1½ teaspoons baking powder
½ teaspoon baking soda
6 tablespoons cold unsalted butter, cut into pieces
¼ cup butterscotch morsels
¼ cup toffee chips
½ cup whole buttermilk
1 large egg
1 teaspoon vanilla extract
Garnish: melted semisweet chocolate

• Preheat oven to 400°.
• Line a baking sheet with parchment paper.
• In a large bowl, combine flour, brown sugar, baking powder, and baking soda, whisking well. Using a pastry blender, cut butter into flour mixture until mixture resembles coarse crumbs. Add butterscotch morsels and toffee chips, stirring to combine.
• In a liquid-measuring cup, combine buttermilk, egg, and vanilla extract, whisking well. Add to flour mixture, stirring until mixture is evenly moist. (If mixture seems dry, add more buttermilk, 1 tablespoon at a time.) Working gently, bring mixture together with hands until a dough forms.
• On a lightly floured surface, roll dough to a ½-inch thickness. Using a 1½-inch square cutter, cut 16 scones, rerolling scraps as needed. Place scones 2 inches apart on prepared baking sheet.

Smith-Byrd House
Bed & Breakfast and Tea Room
victorian teatime

Beth Melling knows the key to making great scones. The secret, she says, is practice. Beth is the scone maker at the Smith-Byrd House Bed & Breakfast and Tea Room in Prattville, Alabama, the business she owns with her husband, David. Located in the historic district of the small Alabama town, the Queen Anne Victorian home, which was built in the mid-1880s, is listed on the National Register of Historic Places.

The dining room of this handsome Victorian serves as the main seating area for the tearoom, but the formal parlor is used for overflow seating, as well as for showers and receptions. Tearoom goers may indulge in The Queen's Tea, which includes a quiche; salad; a three-tiered tray of scones, sandwiches, and desserts; and a pot of tea. Or they might select The Just Desserts Tea, which offers a plate of assorted sweets, along with a pot of tea, among other choices.

Beth grew up watching her grandmother make biscuits, so she knew the basic technique for making scones even before she and David opened the tearoom in May 2008. Eight years later, the Smith-Byrd House's popular Cinnamon Scones demonstrate that she learned those lessons well. They're served all year, except around Thanksgiving, when Eggnog Scones that substitute nutmeg for cinnamon and eggnog for the buttermilk are offered.

"In all of our recipes, we use quality ingredients so that our guests come away with an experience that is hard to find anywhere else in our area," explains Beth. Some of the ingredients, like the Meyer Lemon Olive Oil and Golden Balsamic Vinegar used in the salad dressing, are available for purchase in the gift shop. There you'll also find everything needed to make a perfect pot of tea at home.

Cinnamon Scones
Yield: 12 to 15

3 cups self-rising flour
¼ cup turbinado sugar
½ teaspoon ground cinnamon
8 tablespoons cold salted butter,
    cut into pieces
¾ to 1 cup whole buttermilk
Garnish: additional ground cinnamon
1 recipe Smith-Byrd House's Mock Clotted
    Cream (recipe on page 124)

• Preheat oven to 425°.
• Line a baking sheet with parchment paper.
• In a large bowl, combine flour, sugar, and cinnamon, whisking well. Using a pastry blender, cut butter into flour mixture until mixture resembles coarse crumbs. Add enough buttermilk to flour mixture, folding gently, to form a moist dough. (If mixture seems dry, add more buttermilk, 1 tablespoon at a time, until a dough forms, being careful not to make it too wet.)
• Turn out dough onto a floured surface, and knead gently, being careful not to overwork dough. Pat dough to a ½-inch thickness. Using a 2½-inch round cutter, cut as many scones as possible, rerolling scraps as needed. Place scones 2 inches apart on prepared baking sheet.
• Bake until scones are lightly browned, 12 to 15 minutes.
• Garnish with additional cinnamon, if desired.
• Serve warm with Smith-Byrd House's Mock Clotted Cream, if desired.

Cranberry-Pistachio Scones
Yield: 24

2½ cups sifted all-purpose flour
½ cup plus 2 tablespoons sugar, divided
2 teaspoons baking powder
½ teaspoon salt
8 tablespoons cold salted butter, cut into pieces
1 cup finely chopped dried cranberries
½ cup finely chopped salted pistachios
1 cup plus 3 tablespoons heavy whipping cream,
    divided

• Preheat oven to 375°.
• Line 2 baking sheets with parchment paper.
• In a large bowl, combine flour, ½ cup sugar, baking
powder, and salt. Using a pastry blender, cut
butter into flour mixture until mixture resembles coarse
crumbs. Add cranberries and pistachios, stirring well.
Add 1 cup plus 2 tablespoons cream, stirring until
mixture is evenly moist. (If mixture seems dry, add more
cream, 1 tablespoon at a time.) Working gently, bring
mixture together with hands until a dough forms.
• On a lightly floured surface, roll dough to a ½-inch
thickness. Using a 2¼-inch round cutter, cut 24 scones
from dough, rerolling scraps if needed. Place scones
2 inches apart on prepared baking sheets.
• Brush tops of scones with remaining 1 tablespoon
cream, and sprinkle with remaining 2 tablespoons
sugar.
• Bake until lightly browned, 14 to 16 minutes.

Pistachio Scones with Sweet Rose Icing
Yield: 12

2 cups all-purpose flour
¼ cup sugar
2 teaspoons baking powder
½ teaspoon salt
4 tablespoons cold salted butter, cut into pieces
⅓ cup finely chopped shelled pistachios
½ cup cold heavy whipping cream
1 teaspoon vanilla extract
1 recipe Sweet Rose Icing (recipe follows)

• Preheat oven to 350°.
• Line a baking sheet with parchment paper.
• In a large bowl, combine flour, sugar, baking powder,
baking soda, and salt, whisking well. Using a pastry
blender, cut butter into flour mixture until mixture
resembles coarse crumbs. Add pistachios, stirring to
combine.
• In a liquid-measuring cup, combine cream and vanilla
extract, stirring well. Add to flour mixture, stirring until
mixture is evenly moist. (If mixture seems dry, add more
cream, 1 tablespoon at a time.) Working gently, bring
mixture together with hands until a dough forms.
• Turn out dough onto a lightly floured surface, and
knead gently 3 or 4 times. Roll dough to a ¾-inch
thickness. Using a 2-inch heart-shaped cutter, cut
12 scones, rerolling scraps as needed. Place scones
2 inches apart on prepared baking sheet.
• Bake until scones are light golden brown, 18 to 20
minutes. Let cool for 2 minutes on baking sheet.
Transfer to a wire rack, and let cool slightly.
• Spread Sweet Rose Icing over scones.

Sweet Rose Icing
Yield: approximately ½ cup

½ cup confectioners' sugar
1 tablespoon seedless strawberry preserves
1½ teaspoons water
¼ teaspoon rose water

• In a small bowl, combine confectioners' sugar,
preserves, water, and rose water. Whisk until smooth.

Apple and Date Scones
Yield: 10

1½ cups all-purpose flour
½ cup quick-cooking oats
¼ cup firmly packed light brown sugar
2 teaspoons baking powder
½ teaspoon salt
½ teaspoon ground cinnamon
4 tablespoons cold salted butter, cut into pieces
¾ cup peeled, finely chopped tart apple
½ cup chopped dates
¼ cup plus 3 tablespoons cold heavy whipping cream,
　divided
1 large egg, lightly beaten
½ teaspoon vanilla extract
1 tablespoon turbinado sugar
1 recipe Brandied Caramel Cream (recipe on page 118)

• Preheat oven to 350°.
• Line a baking sheet with parchment paper.
• In a large bowl, combine flour, oats, brown sugar, baking powder, salt, and cinnamon, whisking well. Using a pastry blender, cut butter into flour mixture until mixture resembles coarse crumbs. Add apple and dates, stirring well.
• In a liquid-measuring cup, combine ¼ cup and 2 tablespoons cream and egg, stirring to blend. Add to flour mixture, stirring until mixture is evenly moist. (If mixture seems dry, add more cream, 1 tablespoon at a time.) Working gently, bring mixture together with hands until a dough forms.
• Turn out dough onto a lightly floured surface, and knead gently 4 to 5 times. Roll dough to a 1-inch thickness. Using a 2-inch round cutter, cut 10 scones, rerolling scraps as needed. Place scones 2 inches apart on prepared baking sheet.
• Lightly brush each scone with remaining 1 tablespoon cream, and sprinkle with turbinado sugar.
• Bake until scones are golden brown, 18 to 20 minutes.
• Serve warm with Brandied Caramel Cream, if desired.

Gingerbread Scones
Yield: 12

2 cups self-rising flour
¼ cup firmly packed dark brown sugar
1½ teaspoons ground ginger
1 teaspoon ground cinnamon
⅛ teaspoon ground cloves
8 tablespoons cold unsalted butter, cut into pieces
⅓ cup whole buttermilk

⅓ cup unsulfured molasses
1 large egg, lightly beaten
2 pieces candied ginger, cut into 24 (⅛-inch) squares
1 recipe Sweetened Whipped Cream (recipe on page 117)

• Preheat oven to 400°.
• Line a baking sheet with parchment paper.
• In a large bowl, combine flour, brown sugar, ginger, cinnamon, and cloves, whisking well. Using a pastry blender, cut butter into flour mixture until mixture resembles coarse crumbs.
• In a liquid-measuring cup, combine buttermilk and molasses, stirring to blend. Add to flour mixture, stirring until mixture is evenly moist. (Dough will be sticky. If mixture seems dry, add more buttermilk, 1 tablespoon at a time.)
• Turn out dough onto a lightly floured surface. Pat to a ½-inch thickness. Using a small gingerbread-man cutter, cut 12 scones, rerolling scraps as needed. Place scones 2 inches apart on prepared baking sheet.
• Brush tops of scones with beaten egg. Place 2 candied ginger squares on center of body for buttons.
• Bake until scones are golden brown, 7 to 9 minutes. Transfer to a wire rack, and let cool slightly.
• Serve with Sweetened Whipped Cream, if desired.

The Scone Shoppe
treating everyone like family

Like many new tearoom owners, Theresa Paterno had no experience running a restaurant when she opened The Scone Shoppe in Brick Township, New Jersey. But she had one life experience that has stood her in good stead. "I come from a big Italian family," Theresa says simply. When her parents and all her aunts, uncles, and cousins get together, typically 95 to 100 people are on hand. "If I could feed my family, I knew I could feed the public," she explains.

That feeling of family has carried over into The Scone Shoppe itself, where Theresa's mom, Patricia Cavallo, runs the front of the house. "My mom was always one of the ones who entertained. She has great organizational skills," Theresa says. "She brings such a welcoming face and a great love for people. She's a one-woman welcoming committee."

This leaves Theresa plenty of time to concentrate on the back of the house. In addition to offering 20 different flavors of scones baked fresh every day, The Scone Shoppe serves breakfast, lunch, and afternoon tea. "I do all my own baking and all my own cooking," Theresa explains. "And I hand-roll every batch of scones." For breakfast, that includes omelets, pancakes, French toast, and a ham, egg, and Swiss cheese breakfast sandwich served on a croissant. For just $1.50 more, customers can opt for a fresh scone from the bakery case instead of toast with breakfast. Often, that's all the encouragement they need to come back another day for afternoon tea.

"I always had such a love for entertaining and enjoying people's company, and I found that afternoon tea was a wonderful way to do that," Theresa says. "It's such a relaxing way to have fellowship with your friends."

Pumpkin Scones
Yield: 8

2¼ cups all-purpose flour
½ cup firmly packed brown sugar
1 tablespoon baking powder
½ teaspoon baking soda
1½ teaspoons ground cinnamon
½ teaspoon ground nutmeg
¼ teaspoon ground ginger
¼ teaspoon salt
8 tablespoons cold unsalted butter, cut into pieces
¾ cup canned pumpkin
¼ cup heavy whipping cream
1½ teaspoon vanilla extract

- Preheat oven to 375°.
- Line a baking sheet with parchment paper.
- In the work bowl of a food processor, combine flour, brown sugar, baking powder, baking soda, cinnamon, nutmeg, ginger, and salt. Pulse once. Add butter, pulsing lightly, just until mixture resembles coarse crumbs.
- Transfer mixture to a mixing bowl. Add pumpkin, and mix gently with a fork.
- In a separate bowl, combine cream and vanilla extract, stirring to blend. Add to pumpkin mixture. Working gently, bring mixture together with hands until a dough forms.
- Turn dough out onto a lightly floured surface, and knead gently. (Dough will be wet.) Add small amounts of flour to help work with dough, if necessary.
- Return dough to bowl, and refrigerate for at least 15 minutes to make dough easier to handle.
- Turn out dough onto a lightly floured surface again. Pat dough into a ½-inch-thick circle. Cut dough into 8 wedges. Place 2 inches apart on prepared baking sheet.
- Bake until a wooden pick inserted in the centers comes out clean, 20 to 25 minutes.

Laurel Square Plaza | *1930 Route 88 • Brick, NJ 08724* | *732-899-4070* | facebook.com/The-Scone-Shoppe-194763591687

Gingery Peach Scones

Yield: 16 to 18

2½ cups all-purpose flour
¼ cup granulated sugar
¼ cup firmly packed light brown sugar
2 teaspoons baking powder
½ teaspoon salt
8 tablespoons cold unsalted butter, cut into pieces
1 (3-ounce) package cold cream cheese, cut into pieces
1 (16-ounce) package dried peaches, chopped
¼ cup chopped candied ginger
⅓ cup cold heavy whipping cream
⅔ cup peach nectar, divided
1 teaspoon vanilla extract
½ cup sliced almonds

• Preheat oven to 375°.
• Line 2 baking sheets with parchment paper.
• In a large bowl, combine flour, sugar, brown sugar, baking powder, and salt, whisking well. Using a pastry blender, cut butter and cream cheese into flour mixture until mixture resembles coarse crumbs. Add peaches and ginger, stirring to combine.
• In a liquid-measuring cup, combine cream, ⅓ cup peach nectar, and vanilla extract. stirring to blend. Add to flour mixture, stirring until mixture is evenly moist. (If mixture seems dry, add more cream, 1 tablespoon at a time.) Working gently, bring mixture together with hands until a dough forms.
• On a lightly floured surface, roll dough to a ¾-inch thickness. Using a 3-inch round cutter, cut as many scones as possible, rerolling scraps only once. Place scones 2 inches apart on prepared baking sheets.
• Using a pastry brush, lightly coat scones with remaining ⅓ cup peach nectar. Sprinkle scones evenly with sliced almonds.
• Bake until scones are light golden brown, 13 to 15 minutes.

Pumpkin Scones

Yield: 12

2½ cups all-purpose flour
½ cup sugar
2½ teaspoons baking powder
1½ teaspoons pumpkin pie spice
½ teaspoon salt
6 tablespoons cold salted butter, cut into pieces
1 cup canned pumpkin
1 large egg, lightly beaten
2 tablespoons cold heavy whipping cream
½ teaspoon vanilla extract
1 recipe Maple Butter (recipe on page 123)

• Preheat oven to 350°.
• Line a baking sheet with parchment paper.
• In a large bowl, combine flour, sugar, baking powder, pumpkin pie spice, and salt, whisking well. Using a pastry blender, cut butter into flour mixture until mixture resembles coarse crumbs.
• In a small bowl, combine pumpkin, egg, and vanilla extract, stirring well. Add to flour mixture, stirring until mixture is evenly moist. (If mixture seems dry, add more cream, 1 tablespoon at a time.) Working gently, bring mixture together with hands until a dough forms.
• Turn out dough onto a lightly floured surface, and knead gently 4 to 5 times. Using a rolling pin, roll dough to a ¾-inch thickness. Using a 2¼-inch round cutter, cut 12 scones, rerolling scraps as needed. Place scones 2 inches apart on prepared baking sheet.
• Bake until scones are lightly golden, 18 to 20 minutes.
• Serve warm with Maple Butter, if desired.

• Pat dough to a 1½-inch thickness. Using a 2½-inch round cutter, cut 8 scones, rerolling scraps as needed. Place scones 2 inches apart on prepared baking sheet.
• Lightly sprinkle tops of scones with remaining 1 tablespoon cinnamon sugar.
• Bake until scones are lightly golden, 14 to 18 minutes.
• Serve warm.

To make cinnamon sugar, combine 3 tablespoons granulated sugar and 1 tablespoon ground cinnamon, stirring well.

Sweet Potato Scones
Yield: 8 to 10

1¾ cups all-purpose flour
2 tablespoons firmly packed light brown sugar
2½ teaspoons baking powder
1 teaspoon salt
½ teaspoon baking soda
6 tablespoons cold unsalted butter, cut into pieces
¾ cup sweet potato puree*
⅓ cup whole buttermilk
2 tablespoons honey
1 teaspoon vanilla extract
1 recipe Molasses-Honey Butter
   (recipe on page 124)

• Preheat oven to 425°.
• Line a baking sheet with parchment paper.
• In a large bowl, combine flour, brown sugar, baking powder, salt, and baking soda, whisking well. Using a pastry blender, cut butter into flour mixture until mixture resembles coarse crumbs.
• In a small bowl, combine sweet potato puree, buttermilk, honey, and vanilla extract, stirring well. Add to flour mixture, stirring until mixture is evenly moist. (If mixture seems dry, add more buttermilk, 1 tablespoon at a time.) Working gently, bring mixture together with hands until a dough forms.
• Turn out dough onto a lightly floured surface, and knead gently 5 times. Roll dough to a ¾-inch thickness. Using a 2-inch square cutter, cut as many scones as possible, rerolling scraps no more than twice. Place scones 2 inches apart on prepared baking sheet.
• Bake until scones are lightly browned, 10 minutes.
• Serve warm with Molasses-Honey Butter, if desired.

Preheat oven to 425°. Place 1 medium sweet potato on a foil-lined baking sheet. Bake until fork tender, 45 minutes to 1 hour. Remove from oven, and let cool completely, approximately 1 hour. Peel potato, and discard peel. Place potato pulp in the work bowl of a food processor. Puree until smooth.

Apple Cider Scones
Yield: 8

2½ cups all-purpose flour
⅓ cup firmly packed light brown sugar
2½ teaspoons baking powder
½ teaspoon baking soda
½ teaspoon salt
¼ teaspoon ground cinnamon
¼ teaspoon ground cloves
⅛ teaspoon ground nutmeg
4 tablespoons cold unsalted butter, cut into pieces
¼ cup apple cider
¼ cup unsweetened applesauce
1 teaspoon vanilla extract
¼ cup cinnamon sugar*, divided

• Preheat oven to 425°.
• Stack 2 baking sheets together, and line the top pan with parchment paper. (This prevents overbrowning.)
• In the work bowl of a food processor, combine flour, brown sugar, baking powder, baking soda, salt, cinnamon, cloves, and nutmeg. Pulse to blend. Add butter, and pulse until mixture resembles coarse crumbs.
• Transfer mixture to a large bowl. Make a well in the center of flour mixture. Add apple cider, applesauce, and vanilla extract to well, stirring until mixture is evenly moist. (If mixture seems dry, add more apple cider, 1 tablespoon at a time.) Working gently, bring mixture together with hands until a dough forms.
• Turn out dough out onto a lightly floured work surface. Sprinkle dough with 3 tablespoons cinnamon sugar. Toss dough, and turn once or twice to coat.

> *"A tea party is a spa for the soul."*
>
> — Alexandra Stoddard

Eggnog Scones
Yield: 10 to 12

2 cups all-purpose flour
½ cup sugar
2 teaspoons baking powder
¾ teaspoon coarse salt
½ teaspoon ground nutmeg
¼ teaspoon ground cinnamon
4 tablespoons cold unsalted butter, cut into pieces
2 tablespoons cold vegetable shortening, cut into pieces
¼ cup plus 3 tablespoons eggnog
1 large egg, lightly beaten

• Preheat oven to 375°.
• Line a baking sheet with parchment paper.
• In a medium bowl, combine flour, sugar, baking powder, salt, nutmeg, and cinnamon, whisking well. Using a pastry blender, cut butter and shortening into flour mixture until mixture resembles coarse crumbs.
• In a liquid-measuring cup, combine eggnog and egg, stirring well. Add to flour mixture, stirring until mixture is evenly moist. (Dough will be sticky. If mixture seems dry, add more eggnog, 1 tablespoon at a time.)
• On a lightly floured surface, pat dough into a ¾-inch-thick circle. Cut into 12 wedges. Place scones 2 inches apart on prepared baking sheet.
• Bake until scones are light golden brown, 9 to 12 minutes.

Nutty Sweet Potato Scones
Yield: 12

2¼ cups all-purpose flour
⅓ cup firmly packed brown sugar
2 teaspoons baking powder
1 teaspoon ground cinnamon
¼ teaspoon salt
⅓ cup cold salted butter, cut into pieces
1 cup mashed cooked sweet potato
⅓ cup cold heavy whipping cream
1 large egg white, lightly beaten
3 tablespoons chopped pecans
3 tablespoons sweetened flaked coconut

• Preheat oven to 400°.
• Line a baking sheet with parchment paper.
• In a medium bowl, combine flour, brown sugar, baking powder, cinnamon, and salt, whisking well. Using a pastry blender, cut butter into flour mixture until mixture resembles coarse crumbs. Add sweet potato and cream, stirring until mixture is evenly moist. (If mixture seems dry, add more cream, 1 tablespoon at a time.) Working gently, bring mixture together with hands until a dough forms.
• On a lightly floured surface, roll dough to a ½-inch thickness. Using a 2½-inch fluted round cutter, cut 12 scones, rerolling scraps as needed. Place scones 2 inches apart on prepared baking sheet.
• Brush tops of scones with egg white.
• In a small bowl, combine pecans and coconut. Sprinkle mixture on tops of scones.
• Bake until scones are lightly browned, 16 to 18 minutes.
• Serve warm.

Savory SCONES

Herbs, vegetables, cheeses, and meats are the stars of savory scones. Almost any marriage of these ingredients can make for a delectable experience, from Parmesan and rosemary to sausage and kale. These are all creative takes on the traditional scone that can enhance and enliven a tea menu.

Baking tempting scones to serve is only part of a superb afternoon tea, however. Plating them in an aesthetically pleasing way adds a memorable touch to the table—a variety of dishes, containers, and tiered stands give these creations a unique twist. A basket or a colorful platter delivers a different atmosphere than does an elegant silver dish. Presentation is almost as important as the food, and guests will appreciate the attention to detail as they savor every bite.

SAVORY TOMATO-
BASIL SCONES
(recipe on page 79)

Pimiento-Cheese Scones
Yield: 24

1½ cups all-purpose flour
1½ teaspoons baking powder
½ teaspoon salt
¼ teaspoon baking soda
¼ cup cold unsalted butter, cut into pieces
½ (3-ounce) package cold cream cheese, cut into pieces
½ cup grated sharp Cheddar cheese, divided
½ (4-ounce) jar diced pimientos, drained
¾ cup plus 1 tablespoon cold heavy whipping cream,
    divided

• Preheat oven to 450°.
• Line 2 baking sheets with parchment paper.
• In a large bowl, combine flour, baking powder, salt, and baking soda, whisking well. Using a pastry blender, cut butter and cream cheese into flour mixture until mixture resembles coarse crumbs. Add ¼ cup cheese and pimientos, tossing to coat. Make a well in center of flour mixture. Add ¾ cup cream to well, stirring gently with a fork until mixture is uniformly moist. (If mixture seems dry, add more cream, 1 tablespoon at a time.) Working gently, bring mixture together with hands until a dough forms.

• Turn out dough onto a lightly floured surface, and knead gently 3 or 4 times. Roll dough to a ½-inch thickness. Using a 2-inch leaf-shaped cutter, cut 24 scones, rerolling scraps no more than twice. Place scones 2 inches apart on prepared baking sheets.
• Lightly brush scones with remaining 1 tablespoon cream, and sprinkle with remaining ¼ cup cheese.
• Bake until scones are light golden brown, 12 to 15 minutes.

Butternut Squash Scones
Yield: 8 to 12

2¾ cups all-purpose flour
¼ cup firmly packed light brown sugar
2 teaspoons baking powder
1 teaspoon salt
¼ teaspoon baking soda
⅓ cup cold unsalted butter, cut into pieces
1 large egg, lightly beaten
¾ cup butternut squash puree*
⅔ cup cold whole buttermilk, divided
1 recipe Bacon-Sage Butter (recipe on page 123)

• Preheat oven to 400°.
• Line a baking sheet with parchment paper.
• In a large bowl, combine flour, brown sugar, baking powder, salt, and baking soda, whisking well. Using a pastry blender, cut butter into flour mixture until mixture resembles coarse crumbs.
• In a liquid-measuring cup, combine egg, squash puree, and ⅓ cup buttermilk, whisking well. Add to flour mixture, stirring until mixture is evenly moist. (If mixture seems dry, add more buttermilk, 1 tablespoon at a time.) Working gently, bring mixture together with hands until a dough forms.
• Turn out dough onto a lightly floured surface, and knead gently 10 times. Roll dough to a 1-inch thickness. Using a 3-inch maple-leaf cutter, cut as many scones as possible, rerolling scraps only once. Place scones 2 inches apart on prepared baking sheet.
• Brush tops of scones with remaining ⅓ cup buttermilk.
• Bake until scones are golden brown, 15 to 20 minutes. Let cool for 5 minutes.
• Serve warm with Bacon-Sage Butter, if desired.

For squash puree, cut a small squash in half, and remove seeds. Rub with 1 tablespoon olive oil. Bake at 400° for 20 minutes. Let cool completely. Scoop flesh from shell, discarding shell. Puree squash until smooth. Transfer puree to a coffee-filter-lined strainer. Set strainer over a bowl, and refrigerate for 4 hours. Discard any strained juices.

Sausage and Kale Scones
Yield: 18

1 cup chopped kale
½ cup cooked, crumbled pork sausage
¼ teaspoon ground red pepper
¾ teaspoon salt, divided
2½ cups all-purpose flour
1 tablespoon plus 2 teaspoons baking powder
½ teaspoon ground black pepper
½ cup all-vegetable shortening
1 cup plus 3 tablespoons cold heavy whipping cream,
    divided
1 large egg
1 recipe Nutmeg Butter (recipe on page 123)

• Preheat oven to 400°.
• Line 2 baking sheets with parchment paper.
• In a large nonstick skillet, combine kale, sausage, red pepper, and ¼ teaspoon salt. Cook over medium-high heat until kale has wilted. Set aside for mixture to cool.
• In a large bowl, combine flour, baking powder, remaining ½ teaspoon salt, and black pepper, whisking well. Using a pastry blender, cut shortening into flour mixture until mixture resembles coarse crumbs. Add cooled kale mixture, tossing to combine.
• In a liquid-measuring cup, combine 1 cup cream and egg, whisking well. Gradually add to flour mixture, stirring gently with a fork until mixture is evenly moist. (If mixture seems dry, add more cream, 1 tablespoon at a time.) Working gently, bring mixture together with hands until a dough forms.
• Turn out dough onto a lightly floured surface, and roll to a ½-inch thickness. Using a 2-inch round fluted cutter, cut 18 scones, rerolling scraps only once. Place scones 2 inches apart on prepared baking sheets.
• Lightly brush tops of scones with remaining 3 tablespoons cream.
• Bake until bottom edges of scones are light golden brown, 12 to 16 minutes.
• Serve warm with Nutmeg Butter, if desired.

Salt and Pepper Scones
Yield: 8

2 cups all-purpose flour
2 tablespoons sugar
1 tablespoon baking powder
2 teaspoons smoked sea salt*
2 teaspoons freshly ground black pepper
¼ cup cold salted butter, cut into pieces
1 cup half-and-half
1 recipe Goat Cheese Spread (recipe on page 115)

• Preheat oven to 350°.
• Line a baking sheet with parchment paper.
• In a large bowl, combine flour, sugar, baking powder, salt, and pepper, whisking well. Using a pastry blender, cut butter into flour mixture until mixture resembles coarse crumbs.
• Add half-and-half to flour mixture, stirring until mixture is evenly moist. (If mixture seems dry, add more half-and-half, 1 tablespoon at a time.) Working gently, bring mixture together with hands until a dough forms.
• Turn out dough onto a lightly floured surface. Using a rolling pin, roll dough into a 7- to 8-inch circle. Cut into 8 wedges. Place wedges on prepared baking sheet.
• Bake until lightly golden, approximately 15 minutes.
• Serve with Goat Cheese Spread, if desired.

We used Vanns Spices Smoked Tea Sea Salt (vannsspices.com).

minced thyme, and remaining ½ teaspoon salt, whisking well. Using a pastry blender, cut butter into flour mixture until mixture resembles coarse crumbs. Make a well in center of flour mixture. Add cream to well, stirring with a wooden spoon until mixture is evenly moist. (If mixture seems dry, add more cream, 1 tablespoon at a time.) Working gently, bring mixture together with hands until a dough forms.
• Turn out dough onto a lightly floured surface. Pat out to a ½-inch thickness. Evenly distribute reserved tomatoes over dough. Fold dough in half, and gently knead together, working in tomatoes and adding flour to surface as necessary. Once tomatoes have been worked in, pat dough out into a 1-inch thickness. Using a diamond-shaped cutter, cut 18 scones from dough, rerolling scraps only once. Place scones 2 to 3 inches apart on prepared baking sheet.
• Bake until bottom edges of scones are golden brown, 12 to 16 minutes.
• Serve warm with Smoked Paprika Butter, if desired.

Savory Tomato-Basil Scones
Yield: 16

2 cups self-rising flour
¼ teaspoon salt
¼ teaspoon garlic powder
⅓ cup finely ground dehydrated sun-dried tomatoes
   (not packed in oil)
5 tablespoons cold salted butter, cut into pieces
¼ cup grated pecorino Romano cheese
½ cup chopped fresh basil
1 cup plus 3 tablespoons cold heavy whipping cream,
   divided
16 thin slices grape tomato

• Preheat oven to 425°.
• Line 2 baking sheets with parchment paper.
• In a large bowl, combine flour, salt, and garlic powder, whisking well. Add sun-dried tomatoes, whisking well. Using a pastry blender, cut butter into flour mixture until mixture resembles coarse crumbs. Add cheese and basil, tossing to combine. Add 1 cup cream, stirring until mixture is evenly moist. (If mixture seems dry, add more cream, 1 tablespoon at a time.) Working gently, bring mixture together with hands until a dough forms.
• Turn out dough onto a lightly floured surface, and gently knead a few times. Pat dough into a ½-inch-thick circle. Cut into 16 wedges. Place wedges 2 inches apart on prepared baking sheets.
• Top each wedge with a tomato slice. Brush tops of wedges with remaining 3 tablespoons cream.
• Bake until golden brown, 6 to 8 minutes.

Roasted Heirloom Tomato Scones
Yield: 18

2 medium heirloom tomatoes, quartered
2 tablespoons extra-virgin olive oil
4 sprigs fresh thyme
1 teaspoon kosher salt, divided
½ teaspoon ground black pepper
2½ cups all-purpose flour
2 tablespoons sugar
2 teaspoons baking powder
1 teaspoon minced fresh thyme
½ cup cold unsalted butter, cut into pieces
1 cup cold heavy whipping cream
1 recipe Smoked Paprika Butter (recipe on page 123)

• Preheat oven to 300°.
• Line a baking sheet with parchment paper.
• In a medium bowl, combine tomatoes, olive oil, thyme sprigs, ½ teaspoon salt, and pepper, tossing to coat. Place mixture in a single layer on prepared baking sheet. Roast in the oven for 1 hour. Let cool.
• Gently squeeze juices from tomatoes, discarding juice and reserving tomato flesh.
• Line 2 baking sheets with parchment paper.
• Preheat oven to 375°.
• In a large bowl, combine flour, sugar, baking powder,

Tea by Two
a winning twosome

Erin Bradley and Janet Meyers, best friends since 1982, have seen a lot of changes since they opened their tearoom, Tea by Two, in 2001, but two things have remained the same. "We still like each other, and we still love what we do," Janet says.

Their tearoom in Bel Air, Maryland, is a casual yet elegant sanctuary where people can take time out from their busy schedules to enjoy afternoon tea. Tea by Two has developed a nice following among young adults in their late 20s to early 30s, Janet points out. "They love tea, and they love the experience of having tea at Two by Tea. It's very encouraging because that's the next generation of tea lovers."

The tearoom now offers more than 70 varieties of loose-leaf teas. Guests can enjoy High Tea (soup or salad, tea sandwiches, sweets, and scone with cream or curd), Afternoon Tea (tea sandwiches, sweets, and scone with cream and curd), Cream Tea (two scones with cream and curd), and Tea & Sweets (an assortment of sweets and a chocolate chip scone with cream and curd).

The tearoom's Cheddar-Dill Scone, which pairs well with soup or salad, has a hearty flavor that can also be enjoyed on its own. Tea by Two offers several sweet scones, but the Cheddar-Dill is one of the few—and much-sought-after—savory options.

Erin and Janet also host parties and special events, such as bridal and baby showers. Celebrations like these have a special meaning when the bride or mother-to-be first came to Tea by Two for afternoon tea when she was a little girl. "We kind of feel like the great aunts who are hosting their baby showers," Janet says. "We've watched them grow up."

Cheddar-Dill Scones
Yield: 8

3 cups all-purpose flour
1 tablespoon baking powder
1 teaspoon salt
1 teaspoon ground red pepper
½ cup cold unsalted butter, cut into pieces
1 cup shredded yellow Cheddar cheese
2 teaspoons dried dill
2 large eggs, divided
¾ cup whole buttermilk
2 tablespoons water

• Preheat oven to 400°.
• In a mixing bowl, combine flour, baking powder, salt, and red pepper at low speed with a mixer fitted with a paddle attachment. With the mixer running at low speed, gradually add butter to flour mixture, beating until mixture resembles coarse crumbs. Add cheese and dill, and mix until just blended.
• In a small bowl, combine 1 egg and buttermilk, whisking well. Add buttermilk mixture to flour mixture, stirring just until dry ingredients are moistened and as lightly and as little as possible to ensure a light texture. (If mixture seems dry, add more buttermilk, 1 table-spoon at a time.)
• Turn out dough onto a lightly floured surface, and pat into an 8-inch circle. Transfer dough to a 9-inch pie plate, patting to fill. Score dough into 8 equal wedges.
• In a small bowl, combine remaining egg and water, whisking well. Brush dough with egg mixture.
• Bake until scones are golden brown and a wooden pick inserted in the centers comes out clean, 18 to 20 minutes.
• Remove from pie plate, and cut into wedges. Serve warm.

Tea by Two | 814 S. Main Street • Bel Air, MD 21014 | 410-838-8611 | teabytwo.com

Wedgwood Scones
Yield: 14

2½ cups all-purpose flour
1 tablespoon sugar
2½ teaspoons baking powder
½ teaspoon salt
½ cup cold salted butter, cut into pieces
2 tablespoons minced fresh basil
1 tablespoon fresh lemon zest
⅔ cup plus 3 tablespoons cold heavy whipping cream,
   divided

• Preheat oven to 350°.
• Line a baking sheet with parchment paper.
• In a large bowl, combine flour, sugar, baking powder,
and salt, whisking well. Using a pastry blender, cut
butter into flour mixture until mixture resembles coarse
crumbs. Add basil and lemon zest, stirring well. Add
⅔ cup plus 2 tablespoons cream to flour mixture,
stirring just until mixture is evenly moist. (If dough
seems dry, add more cream, 1 tablespoon at a time.)
Working gently, bring mixture together with hands
until a dough forms.
• Turn out dough onto a lightly floured surface, and
roll to a 1-inch thickness. Using a 2-inch fluted round
cutter, cut 14 scones, rerolling scraps as needed. Place
scones 2 inches apart on prepared baking sheet.
• Brush tops of scones with remaining 1 tablespoon
cream.
• Bake until scones are lightly browned, 17 to 20
minutes.

*Editor's Note: This scone was developed several
years ago for a reception honoring Lord Wedgwood.*

Parmesan-Rosemary Scones
Yield: 12

2½ cups all-purpose flour
2 tablespoons sugar
2 teaspoons baking powder
1½ teaspoons salt, divided
½ cup cold unsalted butter, cut into pieces
½ cup grated Parmesan cheese
3 tablespoons chopped fresh rosemary
⅔ cup cold heavy whipping cream
2 to 3 tablespoons olive oil
Pear preserves (optional)
Garnish: fresh rosemary sprigs

• Preheat oven to 375°.
• Line a baking sheet with parchment paper.
• In a medium bowl, combine flour, sugar, baking powder, and ½ teaspoon salt, whisking well. Using a pastry
blender, cut butter into flour mixture until mixture
resembles coarse crumbs. Add cheese and chopped
rosemary, stirring to combine. Gradually add cream,
stirring until mixture is evenly moist. (If mixture seems
dry, add more cream, 1 tablespoon at a time.) Working
gently, bring mixture together with hands until a dough
forms.
• Turn out dough onto a lightly floured surface, and
roll to a ½-inch-thick circle. Cut into 12 wedges. Place
scones 2 inches apart on prepared baking sheet.
• Lightly brush tops of scones with olive oil, and
sprinkle with remaining 1 teaspoon salt.
• Garnish each wedge with a rosemary sprig, if desired.
• Bake until scones are golden brown, approximately
16 minutes.
• Serve warm with pear preserves, if desired.

> *"The mere clink of cups and saucers tunes the mind to happy repose."*
>
> — George Gissing

Black Olive Scones
Yield: 18 to 20

2½ cups all-purpose flour
2 tablespoons sugar
2 teaspoons baking powder
½ teaspoon salt
½ cup cold unsalted butter, cut into pieces
¼ cup chopped black olives
⅔ cup cold heavy whipping cream
Olive oil
Kosher salt
1 recipe Pesto Cream (recipe on page 122)

• Preheat oven to 375°.
• Line 2 baking sheets with parchment paper.
• In a medium bowl, combine flour, sugar, baking powder, and salt, whisking well. Using a pastry blender, cut butter into flour mixture until mixture resembles coarse crumbs. Add olives, tossing to combine. Gradually add cream, stirring until mixture is evenly moist. (If mixture seems dry, add more cream, 1 tablespoon at a time.) Working gently, bring mixture together with hands until a dough forms.
• Turn out dough onto a lightly floured surface, and roll to a ½-inch thickness. Using a 2-inch round cutter, cut as many scones as possible, rerolling scraps as needed, but no more than twice. Place scones 2 inches apart on prepared baking sheets.
• Lightly brush tops of scones with olive oil, and sprinkle with kosher salt.
• Bake until scones are golden brown, 15 to 17 minutes.
• Serve warm with Pesto Cream, if desired.

Herbed Scones
Yield: 12

2 cups self-rising flour
2 tablespoons chopped fresh parsley
1 teaspoon herbes de Provence or other dried
    mixed herbs
½ teaspoon chopped fresh chives
⅛ teaspoon salt
6 tablespoons cold salted butter, cut into pieces
½ cup whole milk

• Preheat oven to 400°.
• Line a baking sheet with parchment paper.
• In the work bowl of a food processor, combine flour, parsley, herbes de Provence, chives, and salt, pulsing to mix. Add butter, pulsing until mixture resembles coarse crumbs. Add milk, processing until mixture forms a pliable dough. (Be careful not to overmix.)
• Turn out dough onto a lightly floured surface, and roll to a ½-inch thickness. Using a 2-inch round cutter, cut 12 scones from dough, rerolling scraps as needed. Place scones 2 inches apart on prepared baking sheet.
• Bake until scones are golden brown, 14 to 16 minutes.

"I always fear that creation will expire before teatime."

— Sydney Smith

Cheddar-Herb Drop Scones
Yield: 10 to 12

2 cups self-rising flour
½ teaspoon dried thyme
¼ teaspoon dried basil
¼ teaspoon dried oregano
¼ teaspoon salt
¼ teaspoon ground black pepper
4 tablespoons cold salted butter, cut into pieces
1 cup shredded Cheddar cheese
½ cup plus 2 tablespoons whole milk

• Preheat oven to 350°.
• Line a baking sheet with parchment paper.
• In a large bowl, combine flour, thyme, basil, oregano, salt, and pepper, whisking well. Using a pastry blender, cut butter into flour mixture until mixture resembles coarse crumbs. Add cheese, tossing to combine. Gradually add milk to flour mixture, stirring until mixture is evenly moist. (If mixture seems dry, add more milk, 1 tablespoon at a time.) Working gently, bring mixture together with hands until a dough forms.
• Using a levered 3-tablespoon scoop, drop dough 2 inches apart on prepared baking sheet.
• Bake until scones are golden brown, 18 to 20 minutes.

Rosemary-Walnut Scones
Yield: 8

1½ cups all-purpose flour
1 teaspoon baking powder
½ teaspoon salt
½ teaspoon ground black pepper
¼ cup cold unsalted butter, cut into pieces
½ cup chopped walnuts
1 tablespoon chopped fresh rosemary
½ cup plus 2 tablespoons cold heavy
   whipping cream, divided
Garnish: fresh rosemary sprigs

• Preheat oven to 375°.
• Line a baking sheet with parchment paper.
• In a medium bowl, combine flour, baking powder, salt, and pepper, whisking well. Using a pastry blender, cut butter into flour mixture until mixture resembles coarse crumbs. Add walnuts and rosemary, stirring to combine. Gradually add ½ cup cream, stirring until mixture is evenly moist. (If mixture seems dry, add more cream, 1 tablespoon at a time.) Working gently, bring mixture together with hands until a dough forms.
• Turn out dough onto a lightly floured surface, and roll into an 8-inch circle. Cut into 8 wedges. Place wedges 2 inches apart on prepared baking sheet.
• Brush wedges with remaining 2 tablespoons cream.
• Garnish each wedge with a rosemary sprig, if desired.
• Bake until scones are lightly browned, 15 to 20 minutes. Let cool on baking sheet for 5 minutes.

Brambleberry Cottage & Tea Shoppe
celebrating life with tea

What is the proper way to set a table for tea? Dawn Kiki, the owner of Brambleberry Cottage & Tea Shoppe in Spokane, Washington, thinks there are many possibilities. "We set our tables in creative ways, and we don't always do it the same," she points out. "Having tea at Brambleberry Cottage is always a fun adventure; you never know what you're going to find."

That sense of artistry carries over to the tearoom's scones. "We don't like to serve the same scones twice," says Dawn. "We're always creating new flavors." She and colleague Laura Henegar came up with the recipe for Herbed Polenta Scones with Sauvignon Blanc for a local wine event. "They paired us with a winery, so we thought how fun to have a scone with wine in it," she recalls. "People came back to our booth begging for the recipe."

After two decades in business, Dawn has learned a thing or two about running a successful tearoom. She and her mother, Melanie Lenhart, opened Brambleberry Cottage on November 24, 1995. The original tearoom was in a strip mall. "We did a lot of work to make it look like a cottage," Dawn recalls. Then 11 years ago, she found a 1906 cottage in the University District just east of downtown Spokane, and Brambleberry Cottage settled into its current home.

Three tiers of tea service are offered: tea and light refreshments, a nod to the British television series *Keeping Up Appearances*; a special tea that includes scones, savories, and a decadent dessert; and a fancier, high tea served on the tearoom's best china.

"Lots of birthdays and anniversaries are celebrated at Brambleberry Cottage. We have guests of all ages—from newborn babies to a grandmother 103 years of age," Dawn says. "It's just fun to see all the different occasions that people can think of to celebrate with tea."

Herbed Polenta and Sauvignon Blanc Scones
Yield: 16

1 cup Sauvignon Blanc wine
¼ cup polenta
3 cups all-purpose flour
1 tablespoon baking powder
2 teaspoons salt
½ teaspoon baking soda
½ cup grated Parmesan cheese
4 teaspoons mixed dried herbs, such as parsley, rosemary, sage, basil, and fennel
¾ cup cold salted butter, cut into pieces
½ to ¾ cup whole buttermilk
1 tablespoon salted butter, melted
Garnish: additional polenta, additional grated Parmesan cheese

• In a small saucepan, heat wine until it starts to boil. Add polenta, stirring constantly for approximately 3 minutes. Reduce heat to low, and cook until polenta begins to soften and liquid is absorbed, approximately 5 minutes, stirring frequently so polenta does not stick to bottom of pan. Remove from heat, and let cool.
• Preheat oven to 350°.
• Line 2 rimmed baking sheets with parchment paper.
• In a bowl, combine flour, baking powder, salt, and baking soda, whisking well. Add cheese and herbs, whisking well. Using a pastry blender, cut butter into flour mixture until it resembles coarse crumbs. Crumble cooked polenta over flour mixture, and gently fold in.
• Add ½ cup buttermilk to flour mixture, stirring until just combined. (If dough seems dry, add remaining ¼ cup buttermilk.)
• Turn out dough onto a lightly floured surface. Gently shape dough into a ball, and cut in half. Shape each half into an 8-inch circle, and cut into 8 wedges. Place scones 2 inches apart on prepared baking sheets.
• Brush tops of scones with melted butter.
• Garnish tops of scones with additional polenta and cheese.
• Bake until tops of scones are golden brown, 15 to 20 minutes.

Caraway-Dill Scones
Yield: 16

2 cups all-purpose flour
2 teaspoons baking powder
½ teaspoon salt
¼ teaspoon ground black pepper
¼ cup cold salted butter, cut into pieces
2 tablespoons chopped fresh dill
2½ teaspoons caraway seeds, divided
1 teaspoon dried dill
1 cup cold heavy whipping cream
1 tablespoon olive oil

• Preheat oven to 350°.
• Line a baking sheet with parchment paper.
• In a medium bowl, combine flour, baking powder, salt, and pepper, whisking well. Using a pastry blender, cut butter into flour mixture until mixture resembles coarse crumbs. Add fresh dill, 2 teaspoons caraway seeds, and dried dill, stirring to combine. Gradually add cream to flour mixture, stirring until mixture is evenly moist. (If mixture seems dry, add more cream, 1 tablespoon at a time.) Working gently, bring mixture together with hands until a dough forms.
• Turn out dough onto a lightly floured surface, and roll to a ½-inch thickness. Using a diamond-shaped cutter, cut as many scones as possible, rerolling scraps once. Place scones 2 inches apart on prepared baking sheet.
• Lightly brush tops of scones with olive oil. Sprinkle remaining ½ teaspoon caraway seeds over tops of scones.
• Bake until scones are light golden brown, 18 to 20 minutes.

Savory Sun-Dried Tomato Scones
Yield: 24

2 cups self-rising flour
¼ teaspoon salt
¼ cup ground sun-dried tomatoes*
5 tablespoons cold salted butter, cut into pieces
¼ cup grated Parmesan cheese
¼ teaspoon dried thyme
¼ teaspoon dried basil
¼ teaspoon dried oregano
1 cup plus 3 tablespoons cold heavy whipping cream, divided
1 tablespoon coarse salt
1 recipe Basil-Pignoli Cream (recipe on page 122)

• Preheat oven to 425°.
• Line 2 baking sheets with parchment paper.
• In a large bowl, combine flour and salt, whisking well. Add sun-dried tomatoes, stirring to combine. Using a pastry blender, cut butter into flour mixture until mixture resembles coarse crumbs. Add cheese, thyme, basil, and oregano, stirring to combine. Gradually add 1 cup cream to flour mixture, stirring until mixture is evenly moist. (If mixture seems dry, add more cream, 1 tablespoon at a time.) Working gently, bring mixture together with hands until a dough forms.
• Turn out dough onto a floured surface, and knead gently. Roll dough to a ½-inch thickness. Using a 1¾-inch cutter, cut 24 scones, rerolling scraps only once. Place scones 2 inches apart on prepared baking sheet.
• Brush tops of scones with remaining 3 tablespoons cream, and sprinkle with coarse salt.
• Bake until golden brown, 6 to 8 minutes.
• Serve with Basil-Pignoli Cream, if desired.

To grind sun-dried tomatoes, place in the work bowl of a food processor, and pulse until finely chopped.

cut butter into flour mixture until mixture resembles coarse crumbs. Add spinach and basil, tossing to combine. Slowly add cream, stirring until mixture is evenly moist. (If mixture seems dry, add more cream, 1 tablespoon at a time.) Working gently, bring mixture together with hands until a dough forms.
• On a lightly floured surface, roll dough to a ½-inch thickness. Using a 2½-inch square cutter, cut 20 scones, rerolling scraps once. Place scones 2 inches apart on prepared baking sheets.
• In a small bowl, combine egg and water, beating lightly. Brush tops of scones lightly with egg mixture. Sprinkle each scone with approximately ⅛ teaspoon pepper.
• Bake until scones are golden brown, 14 to 16 minutes.
• Serve warm with Cracked Pepper and Lemon Double Cream, if desired.

Parmesan Scones
Yield: approximately 12

2 cups cake flour
⅔ cup grated Parmesan cheese, divided
1 tablespoon baking powder
½ teaspoon salt
½ teaspoon freshly ground black pepper
½ cup cold unsalted butter, cut into pieces
½ cup cold heavy whipping cream
1 large egg, lightly beaten
2 tablespoons olive oil
1 recipe Summer Lettuce Pesto (recipe on page 122)

• Preheat oven to 400°.
• Line a baking sheet with parchment paper.
• In a medium bowl, combine flour, ⅓ cup cheese, baking powder, salt, and pepper, whisking well. Using a pastry blender, cut butter into flour mixture until mixture resembles coarse crumbs.
• In a liquid-measuring cup, combine cream and egg, whisking well. Gradually add to flour mixture, stirring gently with a fork until mixture is evenly moist. (If mixture seems dry, add more cream, 1 tablespoon at a time.) Working gently, bring mixture together with hands until a dough forms.
• Turn out dough onto a lightly floured surface, and roll to a ½-inch thickness. Using a 2-inch oval cutter, cut as many scones as possible, rerolling scraps only once. Place scones 2 inches apart on prepared baking sheet.
• Lightly brush tops of scones with olive oil, and sprinkle with remaining ⅓ cup cheese.
• Bake until cheese is light golden brown, 12 to 14 minutes.
• Serve warm with Summer Lettuce Pesto, if desired.

Spinach-Basil Scones
Yield: 20

2½ cups all-purpose flour
2 tablespoons sugar
2 teaspoons baking powder
½ teaspoon salt
½ cup cold unsalted butter, cut into pieces
¼ cup chopped baby spinach
¼ cup chopped fresh basil
1 cup cold heavy whipping cream, divided
1 large egg
1 teaspoon water
2½ teaspoons coarsely ground black pepper
1 recipe Cracked Pepper and Lemon Double Cream (recipe on page 124)

• Preheat oven to 375°.
• Line 2 baking sheets with parchment paper.
• In a medium bowl, combine flour, sugar, baking powder, and salt, whisking well. Using a pastry blender,

Rosemary–White Cheddar Scones
Yield: 12

3 cups all-purpose flour
1 tablespoon baking powder
2 teaspoons chopped fresh rosemary
¼ teaspoon salt
½ cup cold salted butter, cut into pieces
½ cup shredded sharp white Cheddar cheese
1 cup cold heavy whipping cream
1 large egg
1 tablespoon olive oil
¼ teaspoon sea salt
Garnish: fresh rosemary sprigs

• Preheat oven to 400°.
• Line 2 baking sheets with parchment paper.
• In a large bowl, combine flour, baking powder, rosemary, and salt. Using a pastry blender, cut butter into flour mixture until mixture resembles coarse crumbs. Add cheese, tossing to combine.
• In a liquid-measuring cup, combine cream and egg, whisking well. Gradually add to flour mixture, stirring until mixture is evenly moist. (If mixture seems dry, add more cream, 1 tablespoon at a time.) Working gently, bring mixture together with hands until a dough forms.
• Turn out dough onto a lightly floured surface, and roll to a ½-inch thickness. Using a 3-inch round cutter, cut 12 scones, rerolling scraps as needed. Place scones 2 inches apart on prepared baking sheet.
• Brush scones with olive oil, and sprinkle with sea salt.
• Bake until scones are lightly lightly browned, 11 to 13 minutes.
• Garnish with rosemary sprigs, if desired.

Basil-Lemon Scones
Yield: 12

2 cups all-purpose flour
¼ cup sugar
¼ cup chopped fresh basil
1 teaspoon baking powder
¼ teaspoon baking soda
¼ teaspoon salt
¼ teaspoon garlic powder
¼ teaspoon fresh lemon zest
½ cup cold unsalted butter, cut into pieces
¼ cup grated Asiago cheese
⅔ cup plus 1 tablespoon whole milk, divided
2 teaspoons fresh lemon juice
1 large egg, lightly beaten
1 recipe Lemon Butter (recipe on page 115)

• Preheat oven to 400°.
• Stack 2 baking sheets together, and line the top pan with parchment paper. (This prevents overbrowning.)
• In a large bowl, combine flour, sugar, basil, baking powder, baking soda, salt, garlic powder, and lemon zest, whisking well. Using a pastry blender, cut butter into flour mixture until mixture resembles coarse crumbs. Add cheese, tossing to combine. Add ⅔ cup milk and lemon juice to the flour mixture, stirring just until mixture is evenly moist. (If dough seems dry, add more milk, 1 tablespoon at a time.) Working gently, bring mixture together with hands until a dough forms.
• Turn out dough onto a lightly floured surface, and knead gently 4 to 5 times. Roll dough to a ¾-inch thickness. Using a 2-inch flower-shaped cutter, cut 12 scones, rerolling scraps as needed. Place scones 2 inches apart on prepared baking sheet.
• In a small bowl, combine egg and remaining 1 tablespoon milk, beating lightly. Brush tops of scones with egg mixture.
• Bake until scones are light golden brown and a wooden pick inserted near the centers comes out clean, 12 to 15 minutes.
• Serve warm with Lemon Butter, if desired.

Gluten-Free
SCONES

Many people are unable to enjoy teatime because of a sensitivity to gluten, a protein found in the traditional flour used in baked goods. Nowadays, with so many gluten-free options for flours, this is becoming less of a hindrance. The following pages feature a compilation of mouthwatering scones baked with gluten-free flour, making them suitable for guests who have dietary restrictions. From sweet, like our Dark and White Chocolate Scones, to savory, such as the delicious Zucchini-Parmesan recipe, these scones are incredible when served alone, as part of an afternoon tea, or as a breakfast goodie. Guests may not even notice the difference between these and their glutened counterparts.

ZUCCHINI-
PARMESAN SCONES
(recipe on page 107)

- Preheat oven to 350°.
- Line 2 baking sheets with parchment paper.
- In a large bowl, combine flour, granulated sugar, baking powder, and salt, whisking well. Using a pastry blender, cut butter into flour mixture until mixture resembles coarse crumbs. Add apricots and chopped almonds, tossing to coat with flour.
- In a liquid-measuring cup, combine 1¼ cups cream and almond extract. Add to flour mixture, stirring until mixture is evenly moist. (If mixture seems dry, add more cream, 1 tablespoon at a time.) Bring mixture together with hands until a dough forms.
- Turn out dough onto a lightly floured surface. Roll dough to a ½-inch thickness. Using a 2-inch round cutter, cut 24 scones, rerolling dough as necessary. Place scones 2 inches apart on prepared baking sheets.
- Brush tops of scones with remaining 2 tablespoons cream. Sprinkle with turbinado sugar and sliced almonds.
- Bake until edges are light golden brown, 18 to 20 minutes.

Chipotle-Jack Scones
Yield: 15

2 cups gluten-free all-purpose flour
1 tablespoon sugar
1 tablespoon baking powder
1 teaspoon salt
4 tablespoons cold salted butter, cut into pieces
1½ cups coarsely shredded Monterey Jack cheese
1 tablespoon minced canned chipotle pepper
  (seeds removed)
1 cup plus 1 tablespoon half-and-half, divided

- Preheat oven to 350°.
- Line a baking sheet with parchment paper.
- In a large bowl, combine flour, sugar, baking powder, and salt, whisking well. Using a pastry blender, cut butter into flour mixture until mixture resembles coarse crumbs. Add cheese and chipotle pepper, stirring until combined. Add 1 cup half-and-half, stirring until mixture is evenly moist. (If mixture seems dry, add more half-and-half, 1 tablespoon at a time.) Bring mixture together with hands until a dough forms.
- Turn out dough onto a lightly floured surface. Knead lightly 4 to 5 times. Roll dough to a ½-inch thickness. Using a 2-inch square cutter, cut 15 scones, rerolling dough as necessary. Place scones 2 inches apart on prepared baking sheet.
- Brush tops of scones lightly with remaining 1 tablespoon half-and-half.
- Bake until edges are light brown, 15 to 17 minutes.

Apricot-Almond Scones
Yield: 24

2¾ cups gluten-free all-purpose flour
¾ cup granulated sugar
1 tablespoon baking powder
1 teaspoon salt
8 tablespoons cold salted butter, cut into pieces
¾ cup chopped dried apricots
½ cup chopped toasted almonds
1¼ cups plus 2 tablespoons cold heavy whipping cream, divided
1 teaspoon almond extract
2 tablespoons turbinado sugar
2 tablespoons chopped sliced almonds

GLUTEN-FREE
— *Flour* —

Many types of gluten-free flours are available today, and we have found that some brands are better for making scones than others. In our test kitchen, we have obtained the best results with Glutino Gluten Free Pantry All-Purpose Flour (*glutino .com*), Pamela's All-Purpose Flour Artisan Blend (*pamelasproducts .com*), and Namaste Perfect Flour Blend (*namastefoods.com*). Using other brands may yield different results. Always sift or whisk flour before measuring it.

Dark and White Chocolate Scones
Yield: 12

2 cups gluten-free all-purpose flour
¼ cup sugar
1 tablespoon baking powder
½ teaspoon salt
6 tablespoons cold salted butter, cut into pieces
½ cup dark chocolate morsels
¼ cup white chocolate morsels
½ cup cold heavy whipping cream
1 large egg
1 teaspoon vanilla extract
Garnish: ½ cup dark chocolate morsels, melted
    according to package directions

• Preheat oven to 350°.
• Line a baking sheet with parchment paper.
• In a large bowl, combine flour, sugar, baking powder, and salt, whisking well. Using a pastry blender, cut butter into flour mixture until mixture resembles coarse crumbs. Add dark and white chocolate morsels, tossing to combine.
• In a liquid-measuring cup, combine cream, egg, and vanilla extract, whisking until well blended. Add to flour mixture, stirring until mixture is evenly moist. (If mixture seems dry, add more cream, 1 tablespoon at a time.) Bring mixture together with hands until a dough forms.
• Turn out dough onto a lightly floured surface. Knead gently 2 or 3 times to coat dough with flour. Pat into a 1-inch-thick circle. Cut circle into 12 wedges. Place wedges 2 inches apart on prepared baking sheet.
• Bake until edges of scones are light golden brown, 18 to 20 minutes. Let cool on a wire rack.
• Garnish each wedge with a drizzle of melted dark chocolate, if desired.

Macadamia-Lemon Scones
Yield: 20

1½ cups gluten-free all-purpose flour
½ cup sugar
1 tablespoon fresh lemon zest
1¼ teaspoons baking powder
¼ teaspoon baking soda
⅛ teaspoon salt
4 tablespoons cold salted butter, cut into pieces
⅓ cup chopped salted, roasted macadamia nuts
½ cup plus 1 tablespoon whole buttermilk
½ teaspoon lemon extract
2 tablespoons whole milk

• Preheat oven to 350°.
• Line 2 baking sheets with parchment paper.
• In a medium bowl, combine flour, sugar, lemon zest, baking powder, baking soda, and salt, whisking well. Using a pastry blender, cut butter into flour mixture until mixture resembles coarse crumbs. Add macadamia nuts, stirring to combine.
• In a liquid-measuring cup, combine buttermilk and lemon extract. Add to flour mixture, stirring until mixture is evenly moist. (If mixture seems dry, add more buttermilk, 1 tablespoon at a time.) Bring mixture together with hands until a dough forms.
• Turn out dough onto a lightly floured surface. Knead 3 to 4 times. Using a rolling pin, roll dough to a ½-inch thickness. Using a 1¾-inch round cutter, cut 20 scones, rerolling scraps as necessary. Place scones 2 inches apart on prepared baking sheets.
• Brush tops of scones lightly with milk.
• Bake until edges are golden brown and a wooden pick inserted in the centers of scones comes out clean, 13 to 15 minutes.

Gently roll to a ½-inch thickness. Repeat scattering, folding, and rolling process with remaining ½ cup blueberries.

• Using a 2½-inch round cutter, cut 15 scones from dough. Place scones 2 inches apart on prepared baking sheet.
• Brush tops of scones with cream, and sprinkle with remaining 1 teaspoon sugar.
• Bake until light golden brown, approximately 15 minutes.
• Serve warm with Creamy Lemon Curd, if desired.

Editor's Note: See how-to on page 129, or go to teatimemagazine.com to view a step-by-step video.

Vanilla-Pear Scones
Yield: 15 to 17

1½ gluten-free vanilla beans
1¼ cups cold heavy whipping cream
2½ cups gluten-free all-purpose flour
½ cup sugar
2 teaspoons baking powder
½ teaspoon salt
8 tablespoons cold salted butter, cut into pieces
¾ cup chopped dried pears
1 recipe Vanilla Bean Whipped Cream
  (recipe on page 118)

• Using a sharp knife, split vanilla beans and scrape seeds into a medium saucepan. Add vanilla bean pods and cream to pan. Bring to barely a simmer over low heat. Remove from heat, and pour into a heatproof glass or metal bowl. Remove and discard pods.
• Place bowl over a large container of crushed ice, stirring cream occasionally to cool. When cool, cover bowl, and refrigerate cream until cold, 1 to 2 hours.
• Preheat oven to 350°.
• Line a baking sheet with parchment paper.
• In a large bowl, combine flour, sugar, baking powder, and salt, whisking well. Using a pastry blender, cut butter into flour mixture until mixture resembles coarse crumbs. Add pears, stirring to combine. Add cold vanilla cream, stirring until mixture is evenly moist. (If mixture seems dry, add more cream, 1 tablespoon at a time.) Bring mixture together with hands until a dough forms.
• Using a levered ¼-cup scoop, drop dough 2 inches apart onto prepared baking sheet.
• Bake until lightly browned, 15 to 18 minutes.
• Serve warm with Vanilla Bean Whipped Cream, if desired.

Editor's Note: Please plan ahead. This recipe requires refrigeration.

Blueberry-Ginger Scones
Yield: 15

2¼ cups gluten-free all-purpose flour
¾ cup plus 1 teaspoon sugar, divided
2 teaspoons baking powder
1 teaspoon baking soda
½ teaspoon salt
6 tablespoons cold salted butter, cut into pieces
1 tablespoon minced crystallized ginger
1 cup whole buttermilk
1 cup fresh blueberries, divided
1 tablespoon heavy whipping cream
1 recipe Creamy Lemon Curd (recipe on page 119)

• Preheat oven to 400°.
• Line a baking sheet with parchment paper.
• In a large bowl, combine flour, ¾ cup sugar, baking powder, baking soda, and salt, whisking well. Using a pastry blender, cut butter into flour mixture until mixture resembles coarse crumbs. Add ginger, stirring well. Add buttermilk, stirring until mixture is evenly moist. (If mixture seems dry, add more buttermilk, 1 tablespoon at a time.) Bring mixture together with hands until a dough forms.
• Turn out dough onto a a lightly floured surface. Knead dough gently 3 times. Roll dough out to a ½-inch thickness. Scatter ½ cup blueberries over half of dough. Fold remaining half of dough over blueberry half.

EXPERT *Tip*

Freeze gluten-free scones raw on baking sheets. Transfer frozen scones to resealable plastic freezer bags. Bake frozen scones on parchment-lined baking sheets, allowing an additional 5 to 10 minutes for adequate browning to occur.

Sun-Dried Tomato, Basil, and Bacon Scones
Yield: 12

¼ cup chopped sun-dried tomatoes*
2½ cups gluten-free flour
1 tablespoon sugar
1 tablespoon baking powder
½ teaspoon salt
6 tablespoons cold salted butter, cut into pieces
¼ cup chopped fresh basil
¼ cup chopped cooked bacon
1¼ cups plus 2 tablespoons cold heavy whipping
  cream, divided

• Preheat oven to 375°.
• Line a baking sheet with parchment paper.
• In a small bowl, place sun-dried tomatoes with enough boiling water to cover. Soak for 1 minute. Drain tomatoes well.
• In a large bowl, combine flour, sugar, baking powder, and salt, whisking well. Using a pastry blender, cut butter into flour mixture until mixture resembles coarse crumbs. Add sun-dried tomatoes, basil, and bacon, stirring to combine. Add 1¼ cups cream, stirring until mixture is evenly moist. (If mixture seems dry, add more cream, 1 tablespoon at a time.) Bring mixture together with hands until a dough forms.
• On a lightly floured surface, roll dough to a ½-inch thickness. Using a 2-inch square cutter, cut 12 scones from dough, rerolling scraps as necessary. Place scones 2 inches apart on prepared baking sheet.
• Brush tops of scones with remaining 2 tablespoons cream.
• Bake until edges are light golden brown, approximately 15 minutes.

Do not use oil-packed sun-dried tomatoes.

Chive and Goat Cheese Scones
Yield: 24

2¾ cups gluten-free all-purpose flour
1 tablespoon sugar
4 teaspoons baking powder
½ teaspoon salt
1 cup crumbled goat cheese
¼ cup chopped fresh chives
1¼ cups cold heavy whipping cream
2 large eggs, divided

• Preheat oven to 425°.
• Line 2 baking sheets with parchment paper.
• In a large bowl, combine flour, sugar, baking powder, and salt, whisking well. Add goat cheese and chives, stirring to combine.
• In a liquid-measuring cup, combine cream and 1 egg, whisking until egg is beaten and incorporated into cream. Add to flour mixture, stirring until mixture is evenly moist. (If mixture seems dry, add more cream, 1 tablespoon at a time.) Bring mixture together with hands until a dough forms.
• Turn out dough onto a lightly floured surface. Knead gently 3 times. Roll dough to a ½-inch thickness. Using a 2-inch round cutter, cut 24 scones from dough, rerolling scraps as necessary. Place scones 2 inches apart on prepared baking sheets.
• In another small bowl, beat remaining egg. Brush tops of scones with beaten egg.
• Bake until light golden brown, 10 to 11 minutes.

- On a lightly floured surface, roll dough to a ¾-inch thickness. Using a 2¼-inch round cutter, cut 16 scones, rerolling dough as necessary. Place scones 2 inches apart on prepared baking sheet.
- Brush tops of scones with remaining 1 tablespoon cream, and sprinkle with pepper, if desired.
- Bake until lightly browned, 18 to 20 minutes.

Lime-Coconut Scones
Yield: 15 to 17

2¾ cups gluten-free all-purpose flour
½ cup sugar
2½ teaspoons baking powder
1 teaspoon salt
2 tablespoons fresh lime zest
8 tablespoons cold salted butter, cut into pieces
1¼ cups coconut milk*
2 tablespoons fresh lime juice
1 recipe Lime Glaze (recipe follows)

- Preheat oven to 350°.
- Line a baking sheet with parchment paper.
- In a large bowl, combine flour, sugar, baking powder, salt, and zest, whisking well. Using a pastry blender, cut butter into flour mixture until mixture resembles coarse crumbs.
- In a liquid-measuring cup, combine coconut milk and lime juice, stirring until blended. Add to flour mixture, stirring until mixture is moist and a soft dough forms. (If mixture seems dry, add more coconut milk, 1 tablespoon at a time.)
- Using a levered ¼-cup scoop, drop dough 2 inches apart onto prepared baking sheet.
- Bake until lightly browned, 15 to 18 minutes. Transfer scones to a wire cooling rack, and let cool slightly.
- Spoon approximately 1 tablespoon Lime Glaze over each scone.

For testing purposes, we used Thai Kitchen coconut milk. Whisk canned coconut milk before measuring so that solids and liquids are combined.

Zucchini-Parmesan Scones
Yield: 16

2½ cups gluten-free all-purpose flour
2½ teaspoons baking powder
½ teaspoon salt
8 tablespoons cold salted butter, cut into pieces
1 cup grated zucchini, squeezed dry
1 cup grated Parmesan cheese
1 cup plus 1 tablespoon cold heavy whipping cream, divided
Garnish: freshly ground black pepper

- Preheat oven to 350°.
- Line 2 baking sheets with parchment paper.
- In a medium bowl, combine flour, baking powder, and salt. Using a pastry blender, cut butter into flour mixture until mixture resembles coarse crumbs. Add zucchini and Parmesan cheese, tossing to combine. Add 1 cup cream, stirring until mixture is evenly moist. (If mixture seems dry, add more cream, 1 tablespoon at a time.) Bring mixture together with hands until a dough forms.

Lime Glaze
Yield: ¾ cup

2 cups confectioners' sugar
1 tablespoon fresh lime zest
5 tablespoons fresh lime juice

- In a small bowl, combine confectioners' sugar, zest, and juice, whisking until smooth. Use immediately.

Pecan-Butterscotch Scones
Yield: 14 to 16

1½ cups gluten-free all-purpose flour
2 teaspoons baking powder
¼ cup granualted sugar
¼ teaspoon salt
¼ cup cold salted butter, cut into pieces
½ cup butterscotch morsels
¼ cup chopped toasted pecans
1 cup cold heavy whipping cream
1 teaspoon vanilla extract
Garnish: turbinado sugar

- Preheat oven to 350°.
- Line a baking sheet with parchment paper.
- In a large bowl, combine flour, baking powder, granulated sugar, and salt, whisking well. Using a pastry blender, cut butter into flour mixture until mixture resembles coarse crumbs. Add butterscotch morsels and pecans, stirring to combine.
- In a liquid-measuring cup, combine cream and vanilla extract. Add to flour mixture, stirring until mixture is evenly moist. (If mixture seems dry, add more cream, 1 tablespoon at a time.) Bring mixture together with hands until a dough forms.
- Using a levered 3-tablespoon scoop, drop dough 2 inches apart onto prepared baking sheet.
- Garnish tops of scones with turbinado sugar, if desired.
- Bake until light golden brown, approximately 20 minutes.

Banana-Nut Scones
Yield: 18

2½ cups sifted gluten-free all-purpose flour
½ cup sugar
2 teaspoons baking powder
½ teaspoon ground cinnamon
½ teaspoon salt
½ cup cold salted butter, cut into pieces
1 cup finely chopped dried banana chips
½ cup finely chopped pecans
1¼ cups plus 1 tablespoon heavy whipping cream, divided
½ teaspoon vanilla extract
Garnish: finely chopped pecans and white sugar crystals

- Preheat oven to 375°.
- Line 2 baking sheets with parchment paper.
- In a medium bowl, combine flour, sugar, baking powder, cinnamon, and salt, whisking well. Using a pastry blender, cut butter into flour mixture until mixture resembles coarse crumbs. Add banana chips and pecans, stirring to combine.
- In a liquid-measuring cup, combine 1¼ cups cream and vanilla extract. Add to flour mixture, stirring until mixture is evenly moist. (If mixture seems dry, add more cream, 1 tablespoon at a time.) Bring mixture together with hands until a dough forms.
- Turn out dough onto a lightly floured surface. Roll dough to a ½-inch thickness. Using a 3-inch star-shaped cutter, cut 18 scones, rerolling scraps as necessary. Place scones 2 inches apart on prepared baking sheets.
- Brush tops of scones with remaining 1 tablespoon cream.
- Garnish tops of scones with chopped pecans and sugar crystals, if desired.
- Bake until lightly browned, 18 to 20 minutes.

• In a liquid-measuring cup, combine cream, egg, and vanilla extract, whisking to blend. Add cream mixture to flour mixture, stirring until mixture is evenly moist and a soft dough forms. (If mixture seems dry, add more cream, 1 tablespoon at a time.)
• Using a levered 3-tablespoon scoop, drop scones 2 inches apart onto prepared baking sheet.
• Bake until edges of scones are light golden brown and a wooden pick inserted in centers comes out clean, 18 to 20 minutes. Transfer scones to a wire rack. Let cool completely.
• In a small bowl, combine confectioners' sugar, remaining 1¼ teaspoons orange zest, and orange juice, whisking until smooth. Spoon glaze over scones.

Coconut Scones
Yield: 12

2½ cups gluten-free all-purpose flour
¼ cup sugar
2 teaspoons baking powder
½ teaspoon salt
8 tablespoons salted butter, cut into pieces
1 cup sweetened flaked coconut
¾ cup plus 3 tablespoons heavy whipping cream, divided
½ teaspoon coconut extract
Garnish: unsweetened coconut flakes

• Preheat oven to 375°.
• Line a baking sheet with parchment paper.
• In a large bowl, combine flour, sugar, baking powder, and salt, whisking well. Using a pastry blender, cut butter into flour mixture until mixture resembles coarse crumbs. Add coconut, stirring to combine.
• In a liquid-measuring cup, combine ¾ cup plus 2 tablespoons cream and coconut extract, stirring to blend. Add cream mixture to flour mixture, stirring until mixture is evenly moist. (If mixture seems dry, add more cream, 1 tablespoon at a time.) Bring mixture together with hands until a dough forms.
• Turn out dough onto a lightly floured surface. Knead 3 to 4 times. Using a rolling pin, roll dough to a ½-inch thickness. Using a 2½-inch square cutter, cut 12 scones, rerolling scraps as necessary. Place scones 2 inches apart on prepared baking sheets.
• Brush tops of scones with remaining 1 tablespoon cream.
• Garnish with unsweetened coconut flakes, if desired.
• Bake until lightly browned, approximately 18 to 20 minutes.

Raisin-Orange Scones
Yield: approximately 14

2 cups gluten-free all-purpose flour
⅓ cup granulated sugar
2 teaspoons baking powder
2¼ teaspoons fresh orange zest, divided
¼ teaspoon salt
4 tablespoons cold salted butter, cut into pieces
½ cup raisins
½ cup plus 3 tablespoons cold heavy whipping cream
1 large egg
½ teaspoon vanilla extract
2½ cups confectioners' sugar
¼ cup plus 2 teaspoons fresh orange juice

• Preheat oven to 350°.
• Line a rimmed baking sheet with parchment paper.
• In a large bowl, combine flour, sugar, baking powder, 1 teaspoon orange zest, and salt, whisking well. Using a pastry blender, cut butter into flour mixture until mixture resembles coarse crumbs. Add raisins, stirring to combine.

Delectable
SPREADS

No scone is complete without a dollop of cream, curd, jam, or butter. If serving a plain scone, the topping possibilities are endless—sweet or savory, creamy or fruity. When serving savory scones, consider zesty spreads, such as an array of spice- or herb-flavored butters or Pesto Cream, instead of traditional clotted cream. Brandied Caramel Cream is scrumptious with the Apple and Date Scones, and Strawberry Curd is ideal with Orange Cream Scones. Spreads can be plated in a multitude of ways, from bowls to butter pats and from individual portions to common dishes. Artful displays will enchant guests, while interesting flavor combinations will enhance their afternoon-tea experience.

MOLASSES-HONEY BUTTER
(recipe on page 124)

Strawberry Sweet Cream

Strawberry Sweet Cream
Yield: 1½ cups

1 cup heavy whipping cream
¼ cup confectioners' sugar
½ cup strawberry preserves

• In a medium bowl, combine cream and confectioners' sugar. Beat at medium speed with a mixer until medium peaks form. Add strawberry preserves, gently folding in until well combined.
• Store in an airtight container in the refrigerator until needed.

Goat Cheese Spread
(Pictured with Salt and Pepper Scones on page 78)
Yield: ¾ cup

½ cup unsalted butter, softened
3 ounces goat cheese
2 tablespoons heavy whipping cream

• In a medium bowl, combine butter, goat cheese, and cream. Beat at medium speed with a mixer until smooth, 1 to 2 minutes.
• Store in an airtight container in the refrigerator until needed.

Faux Clotted Cream
Yield: 1 cup

½ cup heavy whipping cream
1 tablespoon confectioners' sugar
1 tablespoon sour cream

• In a mixing bowl, combine cream and confectioners' sugar. Beat at high speed with a mixer until soft peaks form. Add sour cream, beating at low speed until incorporated and desire consistency is achieved.
• Serve immediately, or store in a covered container in the refrigerator for up to a day.

Lemon Butter
Yield: ¼ cup

¼ cup salted butter, softened
½ teaspoon fresh lemon zest
1 teaspoon fresh lemon juice

• In a small bowl, combine butter, lemon zest, and lemon juice, stirring well.
• Store in a covered container in the refrigerator for up to 5 days.

Faux Clotted Cream

Lemon Butter

Apricot-Honey Butter

Apricot-Honey Butter
Yield: approximately 1 cup

¼ cup unsalted butter, softened
¼ cup apricot preserves
¼ cup honey

• In a mixing bowl, beat butter at medium speed with a mixer until smooth and creamy. Add preserves and honey, beating until combined.
• Cover, and refrigerate until ready to serve.

Sweetened Whipped Cream
Yield: 1½ cups

1 cup cold heavy whipping cream
3 tablespoons confectioners' sugar

• In a large bowl, combine cream and confectioners' sugar. Beat at medium-high speed with a mixer until soft peaks form.
• Store in an airtight container in the refrigerator until needed.

Brandied Caramel Cream

Yield: 1¼ cups

½ cup heavy whipping cream
¼ cup plus 1 tablespoon caramel topping or
    Caramel Sauce (recipe follows), divided
2 tablespoons brandy
2 tablespoons confectioners' sugar

• In a medium bowl, combine cream, ¼ cup caramel topping, brandy, and confectioners' sugar. Beat at medium speed with a mixer until soft peaks form.
• Store in a covered container in the refrigerator until needed.
• To serve, swirl remaining 1 tablespoon caramel topping into cream.

Caramel Sauce

(Pictured with Salted Caramel Scones on page 54)
Yield: 1½ cups

1½ cups sugar
½ cup water
¼ cup salted butter, cut into pieces
¾ cup heavy whipping cream

• In a large saucepan with a candy thermometer attached to the side, combine sugar and water. Cook over medium-high heat, until thermometer registers 340° (sugar will be an amber color at this temperature), 20 to 25 minutes.
• Remove browned sugar from stove top, and carefully add butter, whisking until melted. *(Caution: Mixture is very hot and will give off hot steam that can burn you.)* Add cream, and continue to whisk until combined.
• Let cool for approximately 20 minutes before using. *(Caution: Do not attempt to taste caramel sauce until it has cooled completely!)*

Peppermint Cream

(Pictured with White Chocolate–Peppermint Scones on page 51)
Yield: approximately 1½ cups

¾ cup heavy whipping cream
¼ cup crushed soft peppermint candies

• In a mixing bowl, combine cream and crushed peppermint. Beat at medium-high speed with a mixer until medium peaks form.
• Store in an airtight container in the refrigerator until needed.

Brandied Caramel Cream

Vanilla Bean Whipped Cream

(Pictured with Vanilla-Pear Scones on page 104)
Yield: 3 cups

1½ gluten-free vanilla beans
1½ cups heavy whipping cream
⅓ cup confectioners' sugar

• Split vanilla beans with a sharp knife, and scrape seeds into a medium saucepan. Add vanilla-bean pods and cream to pan. Bring to barely a simmer over low heat. Remove from heat, and pour into a heatproof glass or metal bowl. Remove and discard pods.
• Place bowl over a large container of crushed ice, stirring cream occasionally to cool. When cool, cover bowl, and refrigerate cream until cold, 1 to 2 hours.
• In a mixing bowl, beat cold vanilla cream at medium-high speed with a mixer until stiff peaks form. Add confectioners' sugar, beating only until incorporated.
• Store in a covered container in the refrigerator for up to a day.

Creamy Lemon Curd

Ginger Curd

Yield: approximately 1½ cups

¾ cup ginger preserves
½ cup firmly packed light brown sugar
¼ cup fresh lemon juice
3 tablespoons unsalted butter, cubed
2 egg yolks
2 large eggs
Garnish: candied ginger

• In the top of a double boiler, combine preserves, brown sugar, lemon juice, and butter. Place over simmering water. Cook just until butter is melted.
• Stirring constantly, add egg yolks and eggs. Cook until thickened, 20 to 30 minutes, stirring occasionally.
• Remove from heat, and strain into a plastic container. Cover top of curd with plastic wrap to prevent it from forming a skin while cooling. Let cool to room temperature.
• Refrigerate for 4 to 6 hours before using. Store in an airtight container in the refrigerator for up to 2 weeks.
• Garnish with candied ginger, if desired.

Strawberry Curd

(Pictured with Orange Cream Scones on page 32)
Yield: 1⅔ cups

1 (16-ounce) package frozen sliced strawberries
   in syrup, thawed
½ cup sugar
1 tablespoon cornstarch
1 tablespoon fresh lemon juice
3 large egg yolks, lightly beaten
¼ cup salted butter, cut into pieces

• In the work bowl of a food processor or the container of a blender, purée strawberries until smooth. Strain through a fine-mesh sieve. Reserve 1 cup strawberry purée, and discard remainder.
• In a heavy saucepan, combine sugar and cornstarch. Add strawberry purée, lemon juice, and egg yolks. Cook over medium heat until thickened, 5 to 7 minutes, whisking constantly.
• Remove from heat, and gradually add butter, whisking until melted.
• Strain into a plastic container. Cover top of curd with plastic wrap to prevent curd from forming a skin while cooling. Let cool to room temperature.
• Refrigerate for 4 to 6 hours before using. Store in an airtight container in the refrigerator for up to 2 weeks.

Creamy Lemon Curd

Yield: 1 cup

4 large egg yolks
¾ cup sugar
2 tablespoons fresh lemon zest
⅓ cup fresh lemon juice (from approximately
   2 large lemons)
¼ cup salted butter, cut into 4 pieces

• In a double boiler or a medium heat-proof bowl set over a pan of simmering water, combine eggs yolks and sugar, whisking until smooth. (Make sure bottom of bowl is not touching water.) Add lemon zest and lemon juice, whisking well. Cook until thickened, 8 to 10 minutes, whisking constantly. (Mixture should coat the back of a spoon.)
• Remove from heat and add butter, one piece at a time, whisking until melted and incorporated. Transfer lemon curd to a small bowl. Place a sheet of plastic wrap on the surface of curd to prevent it from forming a skin while cooling.
• Refrigerate until cold, 4 to 6 hours before using. Store in an airtight container in the refrigerator for up to 2 weeks.

Ginger Curd

Clotted Cream
with Flower Confetti

Clotted Cream with Flower Confetti
Yield: approximately 2 cups

1 quart heavy whipping cream
1 cup finely chopped fresh edible flowers (such as lavender, violets, roses, daylilies), washed and patted dry, divided

• In a large saucepan, heat cream over low heat. Cook until cream volume has been reduced by half, 3 to 4 hours. (Do not allow cream to boil or burn, but do allow a "crust" to form on top.) Let cool.
• Transfer cream to a mixing bowl, and cover. Refrigerate overnight.
• Beat cream at medium speed with a mixer until thick. Refrigerate until serving time.
• Fold ½ cup flowers into cream. Transfer to a serving bowl.
• Garnish with remaining ½ cup flowers, if desired.

Pesto Cream
(Pictured with Black Olive Scones on page 86)
Yield: 1½ cups

½ cup loosely packed fresh basil leaves
½ cup salted butter, softened
1 (3-ounce) package cream cheese, softened
¼ cup toasted pine nuts
¼ cup grated Parmesan cheese

• In the work bowl of a food processor, combine basil, butter, cream cheese, pine nuts, and Parmesan cheese. Pulse until combined.
• Store in an airtight container in the refrigerator until needed.

Honey Cream
Yield: 1 cup

½ cup sour cream
2 tablespoons honey
1 tablespoon brown sugar
½ teaspoon ground cinnamon
⅛ teaspoon salt

• In a medium bowl, combine sour cream, honey, brown sugar, cinnamon, and salt, stirring until combined.
• Store in a covered container in the refrigerator until needed.

Basil-Pignoli Cream

Basil-Pignoli Cream
Yield: ½ cup

1 (8-ounce) carton mascarpone cheese
¼ cup chopped toasted pine nuts
3 tablespoons chopped fresh basil
¼ teaspoon salt

• In a medium bowl, combine mascarpone, pine nuts, basil, and salt, stirring well.
• Store in an airtight container in the refrigerator until needed.

Summer Lettuce Pesto
(Pictured with Parmesan Scones on page 94)
Yield: approximately 1 cup

¾ cup arugula leaves
¼ cup fresh basil leaves
2 tablespoons pine nuts
2 tablespoons grated Parmesan cheese
1 tablespoon chopped fresh parsley
3 cloves garlic, chopped
½ cup unsalted butter, softened
1 tablespoon olive oil

• In the work bowl of a food processor, combine arugula, basil, pine nuts, cheese, parsley, and garlic, pulsing until smooth and scraping down sides of bowl as needed. Add butter and olive oil, pulsing until smooth.
• Store in an airtight plastic container in the refrigerator until needed.

Smoked Paprika Butter

Maple Butter

Smoked Paprika Butter

(Pictured with Roasted Heirloom Tomato Scones on page 79)
Yield: ½ cup

½ cup salted butter, softened
½ teaspoon smoked paprika

• In a small bowl, combine butter and paprika, stirring well.
• Serve immediately, or transfer butter mixture to a pastry bag fitted with a medium-star tip, and pipe butter rosettes onto a parchment-lined baking sheet. Cover baking sheet with plastic wrap, and refrigerate until firm.
• Transfer butter pats to an airtight container, and refrigerate until needed.

Bacon-Sage Butter

(Pictured with Butternut Squash Scones on page 76)
Yield: approximately 1¼ cups

1 cup unsalted butter, softened
4 slices bacon, cooked and crumbled
¼ cup chopped fresh sage

• In a medium bowl, combine butter, bacon, and sage. Beat at medium speed with a mixer until combined. Refrigerate mixture for 15 minutes.
• Spoon mixture onto a large piece of parchment paper. Using parchment, roll butter into a log.
• Refrigerate until needed, at least 2 hours.
• To serve, unwrap butter, and cut into ¼-inch-thick slices.

Nutmeg Butter

(Pictured with Sausage and Kale Scones on page 77)
Yield: ½ cup

½ cup unsalted butter, at room temperature
1 teaspoon freshly ground nutmeg
½ teaspoon coarse salt

• In a small bowl, combine butter, nutmeg, and salt, stirring until well blended. Transfer butter to a piece of parchment paper. Shape into a 1-inch-diameter log.
• Freeze until firm, approximately 1 hour.
• To serve, unwrap butter, and cut into ¼-inch-thick slices.

Maple Butter

Yield: ½ cup

½ cup salted butter, softened
¼ cup maple syrup

• In a medium bowl, combine butter and maple syrup. Beat at medium speed with a mixer until creamy.
• Store in a covered container in the refrigerator for up to 5 days.

Molasses-Honey Butter
Yield: 1¼ cups

1 cup salted butter, softened
3 tablespoons honey
2 tablespoons molasses

• In a small bowl, combine butter, honey, and molasses. Beat at medium speed with a mixer until smooth, approximately 2 minutes.
• Transfer mixture to a pastry bag fitted with a large star tip. Pipe mixture into desired butter pats. Refrigerate until needed.

Cracked Pepper and Lemon Double Cream
(Pictured with Spinach-Basil Scones on page 93)
Yield: approximately ¾ cup

1 (6-ounce) jar double cream*
1 teaspoon fresh finely grated lemon zest
1 teaspoon coarsely ground black pepper
½ teaspoon fine sea salt

• In a small bowl, combine cream, lemon zest, pepper, and salt, stirring until well combined.
• Cover, and refrigerate until ready to serve.

Double cream, also called Devon cream or clotted cream, is a thick, creamy spread. It is available in the dairy section of some supermarkets and at many specialty-foods stores.

Smith-Byrd House's Mock Clotted Cream
(Pictured with Cinnamon Scones on page 59)
Yield: 4 cups

1 (8-ounce) carton mascarpone cheese
2 cups heavy whipping cream
¼ cup confectioners' sugar
1 teaspoon almond extract
1 teaspoon vanilla extract

• Place mascarpone cheese in a chilled mixing bowl. Beat at medium speed with a mixer until smooth. Add a little cream, beating until creamy. Add remaining cream, beating until stiff peaks form. Add confectioners' sugar, almond extract, and vanilla extract, beating until well blended.
• Store in a covered container in the refrigerator for up to 2 weeks.

Molasses-Honey Butter

Laura's Tea Room's Devonshire Cream
(Pictured with Orange-Pecan Scones on page 35)
Yield: 1½ cups

1 cup heavy whipping cream
¼ cup confectioners' sugar
¼ teaspoon cream of tartar
¼ teaspoon vanilla extract
½ teaspoon fresh orange zest, divided

• In a mixing bowl, beat cream at high speed with a mixer until stiff peaks form. Add confectioners' sugar, cream of tartar, and vanilla extract, beating until very stiff. Fold in ¼ teaspoon orange zest.
• Sprinkle remaining ¼ teaspoon orange zest on top before serving.

Thyme-out Tea Parties' Lemon Curd Whipped Topping
(Pictured with White Chocolate–Cherry Scones on page 46)
Yield: 4½ cups

1 pint heavy whipping cream
1 tablespoon confectioners' sugar
1 teaspoon vanilla extract
1 (10-ounce) jar lemon curd

• In a mixing bowl, combine cream, confectioners' sugar, and vanilla extract. Beat at medium-high speed with a mixer until soft peaks form. Add lemon curd, and beat until desired consistency is achieved.
• Serve immediately, or store in a covered container in the refrigerator for up to a day.

APRICOT CREAM SCONES
(recipe on page 24)

How-Tos

Let these step-by-step instructions serve as your visual guide while you create these impressive and delicious teatime treats.

BASIC SCONES

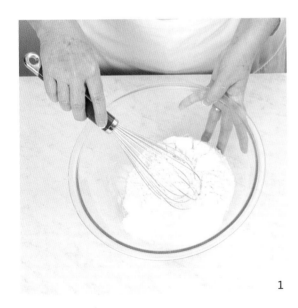

1

2

In a large bowl, combine the dry ingredients, whisking well.

Using a pastry blender, cut cold butter into flour mixture until mixture resembles coarse crumbs.

(Continued on next page)

3

If the recipe calls for dried fruit, nuts, chocolate, or other additions, add them at this point, tossing to combine.

4

Add wet ingredients to flour mixture, stirring until mixture is evenly moist.

5

Working gently, bring mixture together with hands until a dough forms.

6

Turn out dough onto a lightly floured surface. Knead gently 4 to 5 times.

7

Using a rolling pin, roll dough to thickness indicated in recipe, usually ½ to 1 inch.

8

Using a cutter, cut scones from dough. Place scones 2 inches apart on a baking sheet lined with parchment paper.

9

If the recipe calls for it, brush tops of scones with cream.

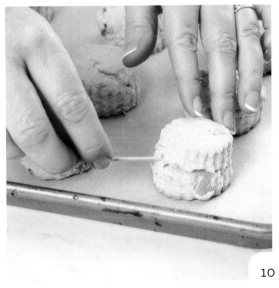

10

Bake until edges of scones are golden brown and a wooden pick inserted in the centers comes out clean.

FRESH FRUIT SCONES

Prepare dough according to Steps 1–6 of Basic Scones How-to on pages 126-127, and then follow these steps before baking:

7

Using a rolling pin, roll dough to a ½-inch thickness.

8

Scatter half of the fruit over half of the dough. Fold remaining half of the dough over the fruit half.

9

Gently roll dough to a ½-inch thickness again.

10

Scatter remaining fruit over half the dough, and fold remaining half of the dough over the fruit again.

11

Gently roll dough to thickness indicated in recipe, usually ½ to 1 inch.

12

Using a cutter, cut scones from dough, gently rerolling scraps as needed. Place scones 2 inches apart on a baking sheet lined with parchment paper.

BLUEBERRY SCONES
(recipe on page 21)

Acknowledgments

COVER
Bernardaud *Eden Turquoise* dinner plate and cup and saucer*. Minton *Riverton* teapot†.

TITLE PAGE
Page 1: Bernardaud *Eden Turquoise* dinner plate, bread-and-butter plate, and cup and saucer*.

MASTHEAD
Pages 3–4: Royal Albert *Old Country Roses* cup and saucer; Spode *Stafford White* teapot†. Maryland China Company *Bernadotte* gold-edged three-tier tidbit tray, 800-638-3880, *marylandchina.com*. Juliska *Berry & Thread* bowls*. Heritage Lace *Canterbury Classic* table topper, 641-628-4949, *heritagelace.com*.

TEA-STEEPING GUIDE
Page 9: Anna Weatherley *Treasure Garden* cup and saucer and *Twigs* 3-piece tea set*.

TEA-PAIRING GUIDE
Page 12: Royal Albert *Old Country Roses* cup and saucer; Royal Crown Derby *Heraldic Gold* teapot†. Heritage Lace *Canterbury Classic* table topper, 641-628-4949, *heritagelace.com*.

PLAIN SCONES
Page 15: Emile Henry *Ruffle Sky* platter, 302-326-4800, *emilehenryusa.com*. Page 16: Staffordshire *Calico Blue* accent salad plate †. Page 18: Maryland China Company *Openwork* three-tier server, 800-638-3880, *marylandchina.com*.

SWEET SCONES
Page 21: Anna Weatherly *Spring in Budapest* salad plate and *Simply Anna* cup and saucer, 732-751-0500, *devinecorp.net*. **Page 22:** Raynaud *Allee Royale* dinner plate, bread-and-butter plate, teacup, and saucer*. **Page 23:** Royal Albert *Old Country Roses* salad plate and cup and saucer†. **Page 24:** Spode *Woodland* bread-and-butter plate†. **Page 27:** Wedgwood *Colonnade Gold* salad plate and teapot with lid†. **Page 31:** Haviland *Princess* salad plate, cup and saucer, and teapot†. **Page 37:** Lenox *Holiday* five-piece place setting, 800-223-4311, *lenox.com*. **Page 39:** Spode *Camilla Blue* dinner plate†. **Page 44:** Crown Ducal *Bristol Pink* oversize teacup†. **Page 46:** Royal Crown Derby *India* dinner plate, salad plate, and teacup and saucer*. **Page 47:** Spode *Stafford White* salad plate and cup and saucer†. Bella Notte Lavender tea towel*. **Page 50:** Herend *Princess Victoria* salad plate and bread-and-butter plate*. **Page 51:** Vietri *Incanto Lace* salad plate*. Holiday spreaders from Mudpie, 678-397-0170,

mud-pie.com. **Page 53:** Smith Glass Co. *Trellis* cake stand in Clear. **Page 55:** Royal Albert *Old Country Roses* salad plate and cup and saucer†. Maryland China Company two-section bonbon dish, 800-638-3880, *marylandchina.com*. **Page 57:** Gien *Filets Bleus* bread-and-butter plate, *gienshop.com*. **Page 58:** Lenox *Winter Greetings* salad plate and teapot†. **Page 59:** Royal Crown Derby *Derby Panel Red* dinner plate, accent salad plate, and teacup and saucer*. **Page 61:** Lenox *Holiday Tartan* bread-and-butter plate†. **Page 62:** Royal Crown Derby *Brittany* dinner plate, salad plate, and cup and saucer†. **Page 63:** Vietri *Incanto* baking dish and *Bellezza White* espresso cup and saucer*. **Page 64:** Godinger China *Regal Cream* square dessert plate*. **Page 66:** Herend *Princess Victoria Rust* salad plate and cup and saucer*. Royal Crown Derby *Heraldic Gold* teapot†. **Page 67:** Bernardaud *Au Jardin* dinner plate, bread-and-butter plate, and teacup and saucer*. **Page 68:** Wood tiered stand from Sur La Table, *surlatable.com*.

SAVORY SCONES
Page 76: Herend *Chinese Bouquet Black* dinner plate and bread-and-butter plate*. **Page 77:** Spode *Woodland* 5-piece place setting†. **Page 78:** Mottahedeh *Chinoise Blue* 5-piece place setting, 800-443-8225, *mottahedeh.com*. **Page 79:** Anna Weatherly *Simply Anna* bread-and-butter plate*. **Page 80:** Johnson Brothers *Eternal Beau* 5-piece place setting†. **Page 83:** Wedgwood & Bentley *Dynasty Gold* 5-piece place setting; Waterford crystal tiered stand*. **Page 84:** Belzoni brown-and-white transferware dessert plate from Mulberry Heights Antiques, 205-870-1300. **Page 87:** Spode *Camilla Blue* handled tray, cup and saucer, and salad plates†. Lace-edge napkins from Sur la Table, 800-243-0852, *surlatable.com*. **Page 91:** Vietri Incanto White striped bowl*. Spode Camilla Blue teapot†. **Page 93:** Williams-Sonoma marbled cheese board, *williams-sonoma.com*. Philippe Deshoulières *Arcades* saucer and *Sully Green* teacup*. **Page 94:** Match pewter leaf*. Pom Pom at Home *Charlie* linen napkins, *pompominteriors.com*. Johnson Brothers *Old Britain Castles Blue* teacup and saucer†. **Page 95:** Annieglass *Roman Antique Gold* oval tray*. Spode *Stafford White* salad plate and cup and saucer†.

GLUTEN-FREE SCONES
Page 99: Spode *Indian Tree-Orange/Rust* salad plate and footed cup and saucer†. **Page 101:** Bernardaud *Saison* dinner plate, salad plate, and cup and saucer*. **Page 103:** Herend *Royal Garden* salad plate*. **Page 104:** Wedgwood *Basilica* dinner plate, salad plate, and teacup and saucer*.

Page 105: Richard Ginori *La Scala* salad plate and teacup and saucer*. **Page 106:** Herend *Chinese Bouquet Garland Raspberry* bread-and-butter plate*. **Page 107:** Spode *Stafford White* salad plate and cup and saucer†. **Page 108:** Royal Limoges *Oasis Green* dinner plate, dessert plate, and teacup and saucer*. **Page 109:** Richard Ginori *Merry Ginori Christmas* teacup and saucer*. **Page 110:** Royal Crown Derby India salad plate and teacup and saucer*. **Page 111:** Royal Crown Derby *Asian Rose* cup and saucer, salad plate, and footed nut dish†. **Page 112:** Mottahedeh *Virginia Blue* dinner plate, dessert plate, and cup and saucer*.

SPREADS
Page 115: Juliska *Berry & Thread* Bowl*. **Page 118:** Vietri *Bellezza White* espresso cup and saucer*. **Page 119:** Juliska *Berry & Thread* bowl*. **Page 120:** Haviland *Princess* dinner plate and cup and saucer†. **Page 121:** Federal Glass *Rosemary-Green* compote and bowl; Anchor Hocking Crystal *Mayfair-Green* handled tray†. **Page 123:** Anthropologie *Fleur De Lys* salad plate, 800-309-2500, *anthropologie.com*.

HOW-TOS
Page 130: Anna Weatherly *Spring in Budapest* tray with handles and salad plate and *Simply Anna* cup and saucer, 732-751-0500, *devinecorp.net*.

ACKNOWLEDGMENTS
Page 131: Spode *Stafford White* salad plate, bread-and-butter plate, cup, saucer, and teapot†.

**From Bromberg's, 205-871-3276, brombergs.com.*
†*From Replacements, Ltd., 800-REPLACE, replacements.com.*

Editor's Note: *Items not listed are from private collections. No pattern or manufacturer information is available.*

SPECIALTY TEA PURVEYORS
The teas recommended in the Tea-Pairing Guide on page 11 are available from one or more of these fine companies.

Ajiri Tea, 610-982-5075, *ajiritea.com*
Capital Teas, 888-484-8327, *capitalteas.com*
Elmwood Inn Fine Teas, 800-765-2139, *elmwoodinn.com*
Global Tea Mart, 888-208-2337, *globalteamart.com*
Grace Tea Company, 978-635-9500, *gracetea.com*
Harney & Sons, 888-427-6398, *harney.com*
Simpson & Vail, 800-282-8327, *svtea.com*
Tealuxe, 888-832-5893, *tealuxe.com*
Teas Etc, 800-832-1126, *teasetc.com*

Recipe Index

Editor's Note: Recipe titles shown in blue are gluten-free, provided gluten-free versions of processed ingredients (such as flours and extracts) are used.

Tearoom Directory